It Wasn't All Mayhem

The Musings of a Matelot

Harry Hargreaves

First published 2005

ISBN 1900604183

Printed and bound in the United Kingdom

Published by Compaid Graphics.
T'otherside, Drumacre Lane East,
Longton, Preston. PR4 4SD
www.compaidgraphics.co.uk

DEDICATION

To my daughters,
Elizabeth (Beth), Heather, Janet and Jennifer.

They have endured my idiosyncrasies,
tolerated my peculiarities and given me
the warmth of their love in return.

CONTENTS

ACKNOWLEDGEMENTS

I have deeply appreciated the help that Judith Sanders of Busselton, Australia has given me through the magic of the Internet. Her advice and assistance on the computer techniques necessary to produce a legible draft were invaluable. Her editing to unscramble the numerous glitches made it possible for me to keep going when I was ready, on several occasions, to call it all off.

The editing was a task of some magnitude due to my rather careless use of the English language. Fortunately, in the family, I had willing volunteers to help with this onerous task. To all of them I must say thank you, your contribution has helped enormously.

I must also thank Bob Hall of Westport who, with his naval experience, produced many reference books against which I could establish places, dates and times. My many friends in Westport who listened to my stories and insisted I write them down are to be praised (or blamed) for the result.

Harry Hargreaves

November 1999

INTRODUCTION

Have you ever noticed that if you take a trip or embark on something out of your daily round of things you can rarely remember the things that went smoothly and well? On the other hand the things that go wrong are remembered in all their sordid details so that in the years that follow they are recounted with much zest and hilarity. As my first instructor used to say when I fouled things up, "Well Hargreaves, nothing is completely useless, it can always be used as an horrible example."

I joined the Royal Navy as a boy in 1933 and left it to join the R.C.N in 1948. My combined service totaled 35 years but in my recollections the time from 1933 to 1945 was a period that made all that went before and all that came after mere details. So much happened in those years that even today I can recall with absolute clarity many of the incidents.

My horrible examples are too numerous to document them all but they have been selectively used to entertain all who have had the kindness to listen. The problem is that the listeners have been prone to demand that I write them all down for the benefit of future generations. I am attempting this task with a great deal of trepidation. The reason is I feel without verbalising them to an appreciative audience much of their flavour will be lost.

I believe that a story containing both humour and tragedy can be told with all the gestures necessary to convey the humour while at the same time the tragedy can be downplayed and left to the imagination of the audience. In writing, the tragedy is barefaced and leaves little to the imagination of the reader. As a result the story becomes a harrowing experience instead of a pleasant interlude.

This may give the impression that all the stories contain tragedy. This is not the case and in endeavouring to put the record straight I looked back to the many situations and incidents that are most vivid in my mind with the thought that among them are stories that should be told. True, tragedy is there; but so is humour and there are, of course, the horrible examples.

The reader must remember that I was 15 years old, completely naive and had been raised in an atmosphere where sex as a subject simply did not exist. The world was a complete mystery to me outside the extremely narrow confines of my home and school. Everything therefore was a learning process. Compared to the youth of today my ignorance of the facts of life would not be believed. I learned a great deal starting with the day I joined.

The period covered by those years were turbulent in the extreme. The Abyssinian war started while I was under training. This was followed by the Spanish Civil war and running along with that were the uprisings in Palestine. Then came the Second World War that affected every living person, not just those in uniform.

In passing I must explain the word "Matelot" (pronounced matlow) in the title. For some strange reason and one for which I have never been able to find an explanation, sailors in the Royal Navy never refer to themselves or other sailors using the word "sailors". They always use the term "Matelot". For example, if one of them is telling a story he will say "I saw these two Matelots etc., etc.," or if you have a visitor while on the lower deck you will be told, "There is a Matelot looking for you." The fact that the word is French for sailor doesn't enter into it. The term has been used in the Royal Navy by sailors since before Nelson and I hope the tradition still stands.

My story is simply that; "My Story". It does not attempt to give a broad account of the war at sea. It does not cover the myriad of details necessary to convey a defined picture of the average sailor or life on the lower deck. There are no torrid sexual scenes of sailors ashore. It concentrates on my experience only and the events that occurred as seen through my eyes.

There is, what may appear, to be a glaring omission. This is the fact that I do not dwell on the many friendships I made during my time in the service; who they were and how we occupied our time. The reason is quite straightforward. A recital of "runs ashore", as they are termed, would be boringly repetitious. How we spent our spare time onboard with the studying, endless card games and the variety of pastimes common to sailors the world over would again be of little interest.

Friendships in the Navy are complex and difficult to explain. When serving together a bond is created between, usually, two people. They interact together, exchange confidences and spend time ashore together; at the same time maintaining a working friendship with the rest of the branch and other messmates. However, the constant moving from ship to ship or shore breaks up these friendships regularly. In the new ship the whole cycle is repeated and affinities are established creating the same bonds with different people. So it goes on and over the years the tenuous links of memory are all that remain of what was once a close friendship.

Under these circumstances my omission is not to downplay the importance of this vital aspect of my life. It is difficult to envisage what life would have been like without these friends; it would certainly have been unpleasant. So, wherever they are, if they read this, please forgive me for not listing you by name and you can be certain I was grateful for your friendship.

Chapter 1

The Navy Way

It is obviously better to start with the very beginning of my career. This was H.M.S. Ganges. Training ships, some depot ships, Specialised schools such as the Gunnery School and the Communication school, all bear the name of a ship and in fact are operated in all respects like a ship. The difference is that they are large barrack installations or, "Stone Frigates" as they are sometimes referred to by those who serve in them.

H.M.S. Ganges was one of these and was the training ship for boys. In the centre of the parade ground was the mast taken from an ancient sailing ship. The mast was 123 feet high and was complete with rope ladders and a devil's elbow. This was the position some three quarters of the way up the mast where in order to reach the next section of mast the climber had to literally hang downward with his back to the ground and struggle on the rope ladders to get on to the next platform. It was a frightening experience for anyone, for boys of 15 it was a nightmare. At least once a week, winter or summer, clad in shorts and a vest with ordinary boots on every boy went over that mast.

On many occasions the ropes were frozen and almost impossible to hold. On these occasions I watched terrified boys being literally forced by fear of the consequences of refusing, attempting to climb. In some cases they would reach either the devils elbow or the topmast then freeze in fear afraid to come down. Immediately this happened two of the other boys would be sent up to help him down. I had to go up and help on many occasions and often wondered what would happen if one of these boys fell. It never happened during my stay there but I am sure it had happened and it was covered up. This may sound cynical but after living in that hell for many months I knew that anything was possible. Today we read of men, in charge of boys, being severely prosecuted for both physical and sexual abuse of their charges. Society was not so enlightened in those days and physical and sexual abuses were rampant.

I arrived at the railroad station nearest to Ganges along with several others who were either on the train when I, and four others, joined it in Manchester or joined it en route. It was quite dark when we arrived and a Chief Petty Officer was waiting to take charge of us when we disembarked. We were put into a canvas covered truck with seats running down the side and driven to Ganges. We passed through the main gate where we disembarked and were "stood to attention" while the Chief reported to the Officer of the day.

The Chief then marched us down what I was to come to know as "The long covered way" to a mess right at the bottom. He turned us over to another Chief on arrival and we were told to enter and sit at the long tables for supper. This was the new entry mess and I found we would spend a month here before being sorted out and going to the different specialized training courses. This month was to be devoted to kitting up, medical inspections, learning the rudiments of marching and generally becoming familiar with the routine.

Some of the boys had been there several days already and were waiting for the last arrivals before starting the daily routine. The pecking order that takes place had already started and one boy had already established himself as the one to which the others deferred. He was a 17 year old from Newcastle. He had red hair, a ruddy complexion and a stocky build. He swaggered around among the latest arrivals deliberately pushing his way through as if waiting to be challenged.

We sat down to supper. All these many years later I remember that first meal. It consisted of a thick pea soup, a chunk of bread (and I say chunk deliberately) and a large piece of cheese. There were knives forks and spoons laid out at each place and at a command from the Chief we were allowed to start eating. Directly opposite me was the red haired boy. I was about to take a spoonful of soup when he leaned over and took my soup and placed it alongside his own, he then took the bread and cheese and did the same.

Here I must digress to explain what happened next. My mother, coming from London, did not speak with a Yorkshire dialect. Naturally her speech became mine and when I went to school I barely understood the dialect that was used around me and my accent wasn't welcomed very kindly. I was different so I found that all through my school years when I first entered a new class I had to establish very quickly that I was not that different and I could not be pushed around. It did lead to many fistfights and as I was not very big I took a beating on many occasion. However, it was drilled into me by my Mother, of all people, that, no matter the outcome, the opposition must always walk away so badly hurt that he never came back and left me alone in future. Believe me it worked, and during a fight I would inflict a great deal of damage irrespective of my own hurt. I used to dread going into a new situation where pecking orders would be established or boys who were in any way different had to suffer the attention of bullies. It could never be avoided so I treated each occasion just the same.

I was now faced with an identical situation. I either had to buckle down and be subservient to this character or I had to challenge him and face the consequences. He was two years older than I and at 15 that is a big gap. I was exactly 5 feet high and weighed 105 lbs and he was 5 feet six inches and weighed a 145 pounds (these statistics were accurate as future events proved). I knew I was in for an awful beating but I dreaded having a future of being pushed around.

I leaned over and put the soup, cheese and bread back in front of me. He jumped up and grabbed me pulling me out of my seat. He then started to punch at me, I say at me because I was dodging wildly. As I rose from the table I still had the fork in my hand that I had stuck in the cheese to put it back in front of me. I then used a tactic that I had often used. Despite his punching I closed with him, hooked a leg around his leg and pushed hard. He fell over backwards and before he could move I was astride him with the fork pushed well under his chin. The fork drew blood although it was just in his skin but he screamed until I told him to lay still or I would push the fork right into him. He lay there terrified and sobbing. "Now," I asked him, "Whose supper is that?" "Yours" he almost screamed.

The Chief, who had stepped outside the mess, returned when one of the boys rushed out to tell him a murder was being committed. He came over but did not touch me, he just ordered me to let him stand up, which I did. He examined the fork pricks under the boy's chin then asked me for an explanation. I was intimidated but I knew I had to carry this all the way so I told him to ask the other boy. He did so and despite the mumbling and pretence it was all a joke the truth came out. The Chief told him to go and wash up then took me on one side. "Do you always play this rough?" he said. I told him that I hated to be pushed around and bullied so I fought back. He said, "With anyone?" and I told him "Yes." This incident was a blessing in disguise. The Chief passed the word to the other Chiefs and Petty Officers and I know it saved me from a great deal of individual problems that other boys had to endure.

Most of the instructors, who were Chief and Petty Officers near retirement age carried a "Stonikee", if that is the correct spelling, I only heard the name and never saw it written down. This was a thick ropes end with a knot at one end and a woven grip at the other. They used these on the slightest pretext on any of the boys to emphasise an order or if catching someone stepping out of line in some way.

It is difficult to describe, much less convey the feeling of fear, and resentment and anger that built up during that training time. It would take a volume to do the experience justice but the water has flown under the bridge, times have changed and these practices have, I hope, been buried with the past. I have often been asked why we did not report these practices and this question illustrates better than any, how times have changed. My answer is always, "To whom?" The realisation usually dawns that the people responsible were also the people to whom such a report would be made. There were many practices carried out that had no other reason than to make you feel how totally you were subject to their whim. Middle of the night searches for illicit contraband in the shape of cigarettes or liquor. I never saw anyone with liquor the whole time I was there but it was used as an excuse by the duty watch to pass the time away. Cigarettes were strictly forbidden but there was a lucrative trade in them mostly smuggled in with the co-operation of the boys from the local village. We had to pay the equivalent price for one cigarette that on the outside we would pay for ten.

Of all the practices however that really hurt was their handling of incoming mail. It was not unusual for them to hang on to an incoming letter or parcel for as much as a week before you received it. All parcels were searched for contraband and the method this particular petty officer employed was to take a knife and cut a cross through the top of the package. He would then fold back the corners and put his hand inside and feel with his fingers for any cigarettes or small bottles. The contents were usually cakes or any types of soft foodstuffs and by the time he had got through with the parcel the contents were a scrambled mess. In addition, if there was something that attracted his attention when he opened the flaps he had cut, he would place it on a pile at his side and keep it for his own use or consumption.

He was a permanent fixture in the mail office, a duty he carried out along with other duties. We had long discussions on how we could get our own back. It was a long time before I hit on an idea and even then I was full of doubts as the repercussions would be devastating. I had been detailed off to work with the naval stores one day and on a shelf I saw a pile of rat traps. They were quite large and of the spring loaded variety. It was winter and I was wearing my blue jumper. I took two of the traps and stuffed them under my jumper. After I had done it I was terrified I would be caught with them but I managed to get them safely back to the mess. Even in the mess we had to limit the number who knew about the plan. I am sorry to say that some of the boys lived in such abject terror that in order to gain some kind of favouritism they would tell whoever they thought would listen about either plans being hatched or who was responsible for some trivial violation of the rules. I confided my plan to a couple of close friends. They said it would never work but finally they went along with me.

The idea was to make up a parcel when we were next allowed out to the village. The parcel would contain some scattered biscuits plus two of the traps tucked in to the corner where they could not be seen when the usual cut was made. We found out it wasn't as easy as we thought it would be but finally we managed to secure them in place and put the top on. All we could hope was that in handling them through the mail the traps would not spring in advance. We had made them firmly secure with newspaper packed on top of them that we knew would be pushed aside when he put his hand in to search. The problem of whom to address the parcel to was easy. Any fictitious name would do as long as the mess number was correct.

The routine was that the mail office would put a card in the mail, collected by one of the mess along with the other mail, telling whoever it was addressed to that there was a parcel awaiting collection. The recipient of the card would get in the queue at the mail window, (there was always a long queue), he would then hand in the card and walk to join another queue at the other end of the building through which his parcel would be handed after having been duly searched. I decided to address the parcel to a boy named Rice who had been invalided out some time before. When the card arrived I picked it up making sure no one saw me and headed for the mail office. It is impossible for me to describe the thoughts that were going through my head as I walked over. I must admit that I was sorely tempted to tear the card up and throw it away.

As usual there was a queue and in the crush to hand in cards I handed mine in. The man collecting them never even looked up and breathing a sigh of relief I headed back to the mess. I would love to have stayed around and listened but I knew whoever was in the vicinity of the mail office would be held as a suspect. I was eating supper when one of the boys rushed in with the news that someone had planted a bomb in a parcel and the petty officer had been badly injured. I knew that the bomb business was ridiculous and obviously a great exaggeration.

However, it wasn't long before all hell broke loose. Five Chief and Petty Officers came rushing into the mess. "Fall in outside all of you", they lashed around indiscriminately with their "Stonikees" striking anyone who was slow in getting up from the table. We left our half eaten suppers and fell in outside. One of them called us to attention, then ordered the boy named Rice to step forward. I had known that this part was a risk; I had to put a mess number to get the mail card so they could easily pin it on this mess. There were 23 of us, 12 signalman and 11 telegraphists. There were normally 12 in each class but Rice had dropped out partway through the course. When no one moved the Chief opened a ledger and started calling out names, telling those called to step forward. He went through all our names until he reached Rice, which was still in the ledger. He called out Rice and I could see the look of anticipation on his face. No one moved. He turned to the boy nearest him and said, "Point out Rice". The boy looked at the few remaining who had not yet been called as if he was wishing Rice to appear. He said very softly "He isn't here sir". "Where is he," the chief demanded and from the back came the shout "At home". A few more questions elicited the whereabouts of the elusive Rice and the frustration was written plainly on their faces.

Needless to say we did not get our supper, instead we were made to run around the parade ground until we nearly dropped. The next day lower deck was cleared and the ship's company fell in on the parade ground. The Commander described the incident in detail and demanded that the guilty party or parties step forward. He then told of the injuries to the Petty Officer. He had suffered a broken little finger and a badly bruised hand. He was taken aback when from the back ranks came a cheer and cries of "Serves him right" and "It should have killed the...."

Commanding officers may be cruel, incompetent, and thoroughly unpopular but they know instinctively when the ships company has been pushed too far. From the boys who, as part of their duties cleaned out the offices, we learned that an enquiry had been held at which the injured Petty Officer had to explain how he could possibly have been hurt in the manner described. The subject was closed and the parcels arrived intact except for the odd inspection when the recipient had to open it in front of the petty officer.

As I have said, they delighted in thinking up methods of making our lives thoroughly miserable. Many of the things they did would be ruled as sadistic today; they used to say it was toughening us up to face life. In my life I have never experienced anything that this treatment made easier.

They introduced a scheme whereby our morning compulsory swimming could be made a torment. I think they had realised that we enjoyed the morning swim. Every morning, rain or shine, winter or summer, at 0600 we were marched to the swimming pool. We had to undress inside and put on a full uniform of heavy white duck. Fully clothed except for shoes and socks we were expected to swim a given number of lengths of the bath. Non-swimmers stayed in the shallow end and were made the butt of jokes as they were pushed by long rods to get them moving. Needless to say, the non-swimmers went to the pool voluntarily in their time off to learn to swim.

The Instructors introduced their new idea intended to make us dread the morning swim. Instead of having the suits dried in the drying room between classes they came up with the idea of hanging them wet on a line outside. It was winter and the clothes rapidly froze until they were almost a solid block.

When we arrived at the pool we were told to collect a suit from the line and strip off and put it on. The trouser legs and the arms had frozen together and we had to pull them apart to get them on. Accompanied by gales of laughter from the instructors we struggled and succeeded then, standing there shaking in every limb, they would make us stand for a long time before letting us in the water. When we did get into the water it felt almost hot to our bodies. This routine gave them so much fun they continued it during the whole time I was there.

Another source of delight for them was the laundry. This was in a building about 100 feet long and 40 feet wide. The floor was completely tiled and around the walls there were fitted large laundry tubs. In the centre were several spinners that by centrifugal force extracted most of the water and the clothes were then hung in a huge drying room.

We were told to strip off completely in the laundry access room then carry our clothes to be washed to the laundry tub we were allocated. The laundry tub was there just to soak and rinse the clothes. We had to kneel on the tile floor with every garment and rub and scrub it until we considered it clean.

The fact that this was totally unnecessary didn't deter them one bit. We could just have easily stood at the laundry tubs instead of spreading the clothes on the floor and kneeling down to wash them. The sight of young boys naked on the floor seemed to satisfy some basic instinct in their twisted minds.

It was at one of these laundry sessions that I encountered the total disregard of those in authority towards the boys. I was on the floor naked, scrubbing a pair of duck trousers that were extremely hard to get clean. They were very stiff and the bottoms of the trousers were black where they touched the boot polish I knew the slightest mark on inspection (yes they inspected our laundry), would lead to problems. I was concentrating and was oblivious to the world around me. Suddenly I felt as if I had been hit with a hot poker across my buttocks. I yelled and jumped up to be faced with an irate Chief Petty Officer I had never seen before.

He had his stonikee and proceeded to lash at me wherever he could hit. I turned my back and he simply went berserk and lashed my back until it bled in places. It stopped and an irate voice was raised telling him that if he hit me once more he would be hit. It was one of the pensioners who ran the laundry and even he couldn't take this anymore. He was armed with a thick stick which he waved in front of the Chief's nose. The Chief eased down then took a good look at me. Believe it or not it was a case of mistaken identity. The boy he was chasing had committed some misdemeanour that had infuriated him and he understood he was in the laundry. The pensioner told me to get dressed and go to the sick bay.

It was here where my last illusions were shattered. I reported to the sick bay and the attendant took me in to see the doctor who held the rank of Lieutenant. I stripped off and now my back was an awful sight. Just then the phone rang and the doctor answered it. I heard him say "Hi Chief" and then "Yes he is here now". A long conversation ensued with the doctor glancing at me from time to time so I knew I was the subject of the conversation. He then said "Don't worry, I will deal with it."

He came over and examined my back and gave a list of instructions about dressings and painkillers to the sick berth attendant. He then asked me what had happened and I told him the whole story. He then said that if I continued to make up stories like that I would be in serious trouble. Why didn't I tell the truth about falling down the concrete stairs outside the laundry room? I told him to ask the laundry attendant but he waved me out. The attendant was pulling at my arm and led me into the dressing station. I couldn't believe what I had just heard and the tears of frustration flowed down my cheeks. The attendant, who was much older, said, "Drop it son, you can't win, they are very close friends".

At the time I did not understand but now I know what he meant by friends. I returned to the laundry to pick up my clothes and met the pensioner. When I told him what had happened he told me not to get him involved. I was left with no illusions of fair play or justice in this place; it was a horrible and lonely feeling.

In order to prevent contraband getting onboard they adopted the most draconian methods. Coming back from leave we had to strip in a room adjacent to the guardhouse and all our clothes, including the clothes we had in our cases were taken and put through the fumigator. We were allowed to wear our shoes and greatcoats down to the mess to get clothes from our kit bag then return to collect our clothes, which were now thoroughly creased, and damp and smelled of disinfectant. This was only when returning from long leave but leave on Sunday and sometimes Saturday was restricted to three hours from one until four.

We were forbidden to leave the main street of the village and our purchases, if we had any money, were restricted to chocolate bars etc. The duty Petty Officer or Chief on patrol would stop you if he saw you coming out of the village shop and demand to see what you had purchased. On return some of us were selected at random and physically searched. Under these circumstances it would appear impossible to get anything, particularly cigarettes onboard yet we did. The methods used varied, but for some reason it wasn't long before they caught someone and another method had to be found. I was convinced by what I heard and saw that it was boys themselves who, in order to curry favour, were responsible in most cases for the method being discovered.

Under the circumstances I realise now it was wrong to really blame them. It made a difficult life almost impossible when you had to conceal everything except to the two or three you could really trust. There was a time when the shortage of cigarettes drove their price up to double the normal going rate. Looking back it seems pointless now to even have worried about cigarettes at that time. I didn't even smoke and certainly I was not tempted by the extra money. The thrill came in beating them at their own game and seeing the frustration when they knew that cigarettes were in the place. They caught people smoking but how were they getting them.

They had just appointed a new Captain to the ship. Through the grapevine we found out that he hated the appointment as it was a dead end with little possibility of career advancement following. There was very little we didn't know as the boys were used as messengers, cleaners and all the other menial tasks that abounded. They heard and repeated everything so in many cases we were forewarned about any changes or action to be taken to make our life more miserable. In this case it was the Captain himself who announced at Divisions (this is the name for a general parade), that all smuggling of cigarettes would be stopped and special measures would be instituted to make sure that we could not obtain a single cigarette. He said that within two weeks he would ensure that not a single item of contraband, particularly cigarettes would be found in the ship.

The Chiefs and Petty Officers and the Royal Marines who were used as patrols entered enthusiastically into the challenge and they instituted some really ridiculous practices. All doors to the toilets were removed to prevent smoking. This was a particularly degrading move, as at our age we felt embarrassed at being in the full view of everyone walking past. They heightened the fences from eight to twelve feet. They insisted that the doors to every mess stand open at all times so that we could not post a look out to warn of their approach and they could walk in unhindered. During the night they would enter the mess at all hours and march through making sure they made enough noise to disturb us. Fortunately they themselves smoked so the presence of the smell of smoke in the air did not reveal that someone was or had recently been smoking.

I must admit I looked on this as a real challenge. Within a week the supply of cigarettes had dwindled and it was obvious no more were coming in. We attended school every day and naturally it was within the confines of the establishment. We had a civilian schoolteacher on the staff, he taught mathematics. He was a pleasant middle aged man who kept himself clear of any of the naval routine, came in, did his job and left. He drove a Singer car that, instead of a trunk (or boot as we used to call them) he had a metal rack at the back on which he carried a rather large box. The parking lot was immediately adjacent to a side door to the school and the toilets were just inside the corridor near the door. I had an idea and while he was in the middle of his session I asked to go to the toilet. This was of course granted and I slipped out of the door and had a look in the box. It wasn't locked; just two push down clips. Inside were some tools and a jack and some cleaning rags. I thought my idea might work.

That Sunday on our rather confined walk ashore I met with one of the boys who regularly made money getting cigarettes for us at twice the normal price of a packet. He knew where the schoolmaster lived and agreed to put a carton of cigarettes under the rags but he wanted three times the price of the cigarettes. I didn't have that much money but I agreed to give him the usual price and if successful would give him the remainder. He said he would do it and the first delivery would be Tuesday. I was banking on the teacher never bothering to use the box and if he did, the cigarettes might escape his notice being buried under the rags.

Tuesday came and I don't think I slept at all Monday night thinking of all the things that could go wrong. I had scouted out the area around the toilets and there was a big hot water heater in a cupboard let into the wall. When I opened the door the dust and cobwebs made it obvious that no one ever visited this cupboard, the heat inside was quite intense. I decided that when I recovered the cigarettes this was where I would keep them hidden and only bring out a packet at a time to distribute. We were marched to school and dispersed at the door to go to our different classes. Some of us headed straight for the toilets before going to class. I waited until the last one had gone then rushed out to the car and opened the box. Sure enough the cigarettes were there, well concealed under the rags. It took just a moment to get them, close the lid and back into the corridor. I pushed them into the heater cupboard and later on went to the toilet and split up the carton hiding them, except for one pack behind the heater. The package was a problem so I had to tear it up and flush it down the toilet and this took time. On future occasions I tucked the empty carton under my jumper and disposed of it under the gash (garbage) containers.

A few days later at Divisions the Captain announced triumphantly that all contraband including cigarettes had been stopped and congratulated the Officers and Instructors on their efficiency. I did not know quite what to do as, in order to ensure no one leaked the fact that cigarettes were available I had to disperse them through known and trusted boys who, if caught would not reveal their source. While I knew I had won the battle it was no fun the enemy thinking they had won.

I pondered over this for a day or two. The dais from which the Captain overlooked the divisions was always in place and it seemed to me the best place to start. I collected cigarette butts from the boys that did smoke and put them in an empty cigarette packet. We were detailed off to clean the dais every morning before divisions and the day came when I was detailed. The Petty Officer in charge never inspected the dais after it had been cleaned as this would have meant him climbing several steps, a fact I had noticed. I busily cleaned the dais then returned to the rest of the working party. The Petty Officer did not have a clue who he had sent over to do the job, it was a case of from here to the left sweep the dais and from here to the right lay the carpet. Admittedly it was a risk but it was worth it.

The parade was fallen in and the Captain mounted the steps to the dais. The cigarette butts were spread far and wide and I am sure, being a large fat man with a very red face, he almost had a heart attack. He called the duty officer up and waved his arm around while shouting furiously. I wish I could have heard what he said. The duty officer called the Petty Officer and so it went but they never solved the problem. Life was pretty miserable for all of us for a few days but our instructor, who was one of the few decent men, told us that the Captain had admitted defeat and removed all the special measures as a waste of time. My source of supply continued until the day I left. I never turned it over to anyone as all my friends left with me and I could not trust the newcomers. Maybe the boys in the village briefed them, not wanting their source of funds to dry up. I don't know but I was satisfied that there is always a way to beat the odds.

Our thoughts were constantly on the day when we would leave all this behind. In our innocence we thought then our problems would all be over. The day came and we were dispersed throughout the fleet. Being boys we could only serve in Battleships and Cruisers. I was sent to H.M.S. Barham, a battleship. I was fortunate in that three of my friends went with me.

Chapter 2

First Posting

We arrived onboard and found ourselves in a world so totally strange we were like bewildered sheep. We had been issued with hammocks on leaving Ganges. We had never slept in a hammock although through many weary evenings we had to hand make the clews and lashings essential for slinging a hammock. We were marched along the upper deck and then down to the boys' mess deck. We were given lockers and told where to stow our hammocks. We were allocated hammock hooks where we had to sling the hammocks at night. Mine turned out to be right alongside a vent exhaust from the ship's galley. The smell of cooking flowed through this twenty four hours a day and if you wanted to know what was for dinner all you had to do was smell me. It was sickening but the idea of complaining never entered my head. I was truly conditioned by the Ganges treatment.

Although living in the same mess we were now allocated to the part of ship and the branch for which we were trained. I was trained in signals so reported to the Chief Yeoman of Signals for allocation of duties. I was terrified of him at first and called him Sir at every turn. That first day he told me quite firmly that I had to address him as Chief and turned me over to a Petty Officer who was in charge of allocating duty watches. These two men seemed quite human and I wondered, cynically, if this was just an act for the first day. It turned out that these men represented the great majority of Chief and Petty Officers. The Chiefs and Petty Officers in Ganges I soon found out were the misfits. Sent there to get rid of them until they retired. The Navy obviously did not know, or did not care about the terrible injustice they were wreaking on the boys who passed through their hands.

An example of pushing misfits aside into jobs where thought they could do no harm was the Petty Officer in charge of the boys' mess deck. His name was Snub Pollard, why they called him snub I will never know but then I don't know why they call all Whites "Knocker" or all Clarks "Nobby". He had just joined the ship, having been in hospital for several months. I suppose they thought this was a nice easy job. He hated it and he took his hate out on the boys, particularly the signal boys.

The routine for the signal boys was such that they kept watches even in harbour. This meant that, in many cases the watch overlapped the meal times and our meals were supposed to arrive in the mess with everyone else's but put on one side in a hot cupboard until we came down. They were never there although the duty boys swore that before leaving the mess deck they had put them in the cupboard. It was a mystery but try as we could we couldn't solve it.

After a week onboard the Chief was walking up and down the flag deck having his afternoon smoke. He stopped and asked me how I and the other boys were doing. Based on bitter experience I hesitated to answer and he realised there was a problem. Finally I told him about our meals. I told him we were averaging one meal a day depending on the watch we were keeping. He questioned me closely and I told him how the other boys swore they had put the meals in the cupboard .

He called over a Leading Signalman and they had a quiet discussion. It turned out that this man was in the next mess deck to the boys and although separated by a bulkhead he could see through the door on to our mess deck. After meals our mess deck was completely cleared leaving only Snub Pollard behind.

It was totally usual for watch keepers coming off watch to lie on the lockers or benches and sleep in the afternoon. This Leading Signalman went off watch the following day and lay on a bench pretending to sleep but all the time watching the hot cupboard. He saw our meals being put in the cupboard. The mess deck was then cleared and to his astonishment he saw Snub Pollard go to the cupboard, pull out the meals and throw them in the, what was called, the "Gash" bucket.

He went to the Chief's mess and reported what he had seen to the Chief Yeoman. All hell broke loose. Snub Pollard when taken before the Officer of the Watch by the Master at Arms with the Chief Yeoman pressing the charges, went berserk. First he denied everything and then rambled on about the people in the signal branch who thought they were better than everyone else and should not be waited on by seamen.

The Officer of the Watch in a side comment to the Master at Arms inadvertently opened the floodgates. He commented that it did not make any sense and at this Snub Pollard, foaming at the mouth, said, "Don't accuse me of being insane, I have documents here to prove I am as sane as you". It turned out that the months he had spent in hospital were in the psychiatric ward and the certificate he carried everywhere was his discharge certificate from the hospital saying he was fit for normal duties. This is the man they put in charge of boys. He was sent back to hospital but I have always wondered how many in Ganges carried a certificate saying they were sane.

I learned a great deal in H.M.S. Barham. We did prolonged exercises during the spring, visiting the West Indies and many other places. It was there I heard and saw naval gunfire in action for the first time during exercises. You have to experience it to believe what it is like in a battleship when all turrets are trained on a target and fired in a broadside. The ship seems to move sideways, she lists over to the side opposite to the gunfire and the noise is hellish.

The days of ear pads and ear protectors had not been reached and it took hours before you could hear a normal voice. We lived a very full life with little time to ourselves. In fact, the only time we were free was one "dog" watch each day; that is from 4 to 6 or from 6 to 8 in the evening. We attended instruction every morning from 8 to 1230 and that instruction took the form of communication instruction or navigation etc with formal school thrown in. We carried a schoolteacher who held the rank of Lieutenant for the formal schooling; everything else came from the specialists.

H.M.S. Barham went into dock for her annual refit and repair and we were transferred to H.M.S. Royal Sovereign another battleship. The routine was much the same as before except we were now expected to do night watches. This meant from 8 to midnight or midnight to 4 or 4 to 8 in the morning. We were not allowed to make up for the hours of sleep lost by sleeping in the afternoon or forenoon like the other watch keepers. We had to maintain a full day of instruction and being on watch as well. The ship did her spring cruise and we went through all the same exercises. Slowly we had lost our fear and distrust of the Chief and Petty Officers. We were treated fairly and firmly but the sadism we had experienced was not present in any way.

The day arrived when instead of being sent from ship to ship like so many sheep we became personalities of our own. That is, instead of a message reading, transfer two signal boys; we were referred to by name. This meant that somewhere in some depot or admiralty itself they had created a draft card with my name on it and from now on my life would be governed by that card.

CHAPTER THREE

On Parade

It was May 1936, I was seventeen and had recently arrived onboard H.M.S. Devonshire, a county class cruiser. This ship bore a proud tradition. Previous warships with the same name had been in battle in all the wars going back to before the Armada. On the superstructure of her quarterdeck was mounted the names of the battles her predecessors had fought and they covered every inch of available space.

Under the quarterdeck in the lobby outside the sumptuous cabin occupied by the Captain there was a huge glass display case containing what was reputed to be Drake's drum. This was the drum with which Drake rallied the ships of his fleet. This was the drum made famous in song and poetry that tell of how the sound of Drake's drum made the enemy flee in fear and brought his fleet into action like a stirring battle cry. This was the drum that all the ship's companies since Drake have regarded as unlucky. Bowing to this superstition or because it was too precious an object to risk at sea, the drum was ceremoniously handed over whenever the ship was leaving on a long commission taking her from her home port of Plymouth for many months.

The day had arrived for this hand over. Needless to say this called for all the bells and whistles the Navy can produce for such a ceremony. I had been told by the old hands that the quarterdeck would be a sight to behold with the marine guard and band in their pith helmets, the ship's company in their number ones and the officers dressed as no other officers in the world could dress. Gold braid down the side of their trousers, swords hanging loosely by their sides and a couple of very senior officers with cocked hats to go with their frock coats.

On the jetty they expected distinguished visitors of every service together with a couple of visiting Admirals who had signalled their intention to be present on the jetty as the best place to see the ceremony. The space for the Admirals had been duly marked and next to it a space had been allocated for the "Ladies of Devon". These were the ladies who by tradition had adopted the Devonshire as their ship and were responsible for many social activities for the officers and the ship's company.

This, however, was a very special occasion, for, in addition to transferring the drum to their care and custody, the ladies had, by hand, sewn together a magnificent white ensign made of silk, which they had presented, and was to be hoisted that morning at the colours ceremony. This ceremony of hoisting the colours with appropriate pomp when alongside goes back far in Naval tradition. For purposes of uniformity throughout the fleet the time of hoisting is promulgated by the senior officer present. This is normally at eight in the morning in the summer and nine during the winter. In order not to inconvenience the "Ladies of Devon" too much, the ceremony had been set for nine o'clock.

As a signal boy I had to keep watches on the flag deck and on this day I had the forenoon watch that starts at eight. As the dress of the day had been piped as number one's I was in my best uniform but the only way anyone could tell was that the pair of flags I wore on my right arm were in gold instead of red. I had looked forward to watching this impressive ceremony from the flag deck instead of being fallen in with the rest of the ship's company. I could see that already on the jetty there was quite a crowd pushing and shoving their way to the unreserved areas.

My day was rudely shattered when the Chief Yeoman of Signals, (to me a personage who at least sat at God's right hand) called me over. "You and Leading Signalman Kettler will be the colour party this morning." I couldn't believe it. No one could be so cruel, no one could possibly expect a 17-year-old boy to stand and hoist an ensign with every eye in the world upon him. He could and he did. I looked over at the Leading Signalman; he was wearing three gold badges under the gold anchor. On his chest he had a row of medals, I found out he had been a boy in the Navy at the beginning of the First World War. He looked totally unperturbed as if he did this every day. I know my knees trembled, I know I desperately searched for an excuse to get out of it, I know that my wits deserted me and I found myself saying, "Yes Chief".

Kettler with a twitch of his head signified I should follow him. He headed down to the signal office under the flag deck and there he picked up the biggest ensign I have ever seen. He handed it to me and I could barely get my arms round it. The silk slipped and moved so I had to grip a fold of it to keep it secure. We headed down the starboard locker on our way to the quarterdeck. Kettler decided to head aft through the mess decks and come out on the quarterdeck where we could go aft and prepare the ensign for hoisting. This preparation consists of clipping the head of the ensign to the halyard on the ensign staff then lacing the ensign through specially positioned holes, then around the mast. This keeps the ensign firmly backed against the mast so that there is no space between the ensign and the ensign staff. It takes time and with an ensign as large as this Kettler wanted to give us plenty of time.

We arrived at the bulkhead door to go onto the quarterdeck. It was early and the ship's company and marine band with all the dignitaries had not taken up position although the crowd on the jetty was quite large. As we stepped on to the quarterdeck, a Gunner, that is a warrant officer who has risen to this dizzy height from being a Gunner's mate on the lower deck, intercepted us. "Where do you think you two are going?" Kettler explained. "No one is allowed on the quarter deck until it is piped." Kettler protested, he tried to explain, he pointed out the size of the ensign; it was no good. We stood there waiting and the Gunner walked away towards the stern. Kettler turned, beckoned me to follow him and headed across to the starboard door. He opened it, looked out all round and waved me to follow him. We hadn't taken four steps when a stentorian bellow demanded to know what the h...we thought we were doing. Kettler said he thought the Gunner meant the port side was out of bounds until after the ship's company was piped. When you have three badges and a row of medals plus standing somewhat over six feet even a Gunner won't call you a liar. All he did was order us back inside.

Kettler asked me if I had ever been colour party before. I told him I hadn't; I had only just joined the ship. He groaned then he explained to me what I was supposed to do and how to do it. His first words were, "When you get outside the guard rail", I stopped him then and there and demanded an explanation of why I had to get outside the guard-rail. He explained that the guard-rail finished about three feet from the pointed stern, the ensign staff was right at the stern.

I had to stand between the ensign staff and the guard-rail and lash the ensign to the staff. "But there will be nothing between me and the water", I protested. "That's right", he said and proceeded to give me a lesson on how to lash the ensign to the mast. "Where will you be", I wanted to know. "Don't worry, I'll be right behind you inside the guard rail, there is not enough room for two people out there on that small triangle". "Why don't you lash the ensign on?" I must admit that I said this with a great deal of trepidation, at this stage in my career a Leading Signalman was right up there just below the Chief Yeoman, particularly one with three badges and a row of medals. Fortunately he didn't get annoyed, he simply stated that lashing the ensign and hoisting it was a boy's job.

It was then we heard the pipe, "Clear lower deck, hands muster for divisions". We saw the Marine band moving aft with all their instruments. "Here we go," he said and we headed back to the ensign staff. I climbed over the guard rail and found the halyards on the ensign staff hopelessly snarled. Some idiot had clipped the ends together then hoisted them until the clips had jammed in the roller at the top of the staff. I pulled and tugged but they wouldn't come down. We were both helpless. I handed Kettler a loop of the halyard to see if he could get it down but it defied his best efforts. We looked at one another; he kept muttering, "That bloody Gunner," as he tugged and pulled.

All around us, totally oblivious to our efforts the marines were formed up, the ship's company fallen in by divisions and I heard the Commander report in a loud voice to the Captain that all was ready. The crowd on the dockside was very quiet as they waited for the ceremony to begin. An Admiral surrounded by his retinue was the closest to us and out of the corner of my eye I could see he was watching our efforts with intense interest. Suddenly the halyard, in response to a despairing jerk by Kettler, came loose. He handed me the halyard and I rapidly hauled it round so I could get hold of the clips.

He handed me the ensign and I realised with a sinking heart that this huge mass of slippery silk needed both hands to hold it with no possibility of finding the head of the ensign to clip it on before I could start lashing it on. Kettler saw my predicament and leaned over to help. The routine is that a signalman standing by the ship's Bell strikes it for the appropriate hour, (I never understood why this duty fell to a signalman when at all other times the quartermaster carries out this task). On hearing the bell the bugler sounds the "Still". The Bell rang out and the bugler sounded the Still. We looked at one another and Kettler said, "To Hell with the lashing, just bend it on".

I grabbed at the ensign, then how it happened I don't know, I dropped it. I grabbed at it but only made things worse as by hitting it, it unfolded. I watched in terrified fascination as it dropped. Before it hit the filthy oil covered water the breeze caught it and it spread out and rested on the surface of the water. If I close my eyes and listen I can still hear the groan from the assembled throng. The bandmaster with his back to us was totally oblivious to the situation and with a wave of his baton started the band into the national anthem. Kettler and I stood rigid facing the ensign staff and watched the ensign gently floating away on the tide. The National Anthem seemed to take ages. All the officers both onboard and onshore were standing in rigid salute. Civilians had removed their hats. The Marine Colour Guard was presenting arms. Everyone of them was facing the ensign staff. I was in a state of petrified terror. The Leading Signalman stood at the salute facing aft and seemed completely unperturbed.

The bugle signalled the end and out on the quarterdeck keeping to the guard-rail came a signalman with an ensign tucked under his arm. Kettler handed it to me and with hands that could barely stop shaking, I laced it on and we hoisted it slowly and with dignity. Meanwhile, the officer of the watch had called away a boat to recover the ensign, which they did in remarkably quick time. I climbed back inboard to be faced with the Chief Yeoman and the Master at Arms. The Marines were marched away as we watched and soon the quarterdeck was clear of the ceremonious assembly

The Leading Signalman and I were hustled into the quarter deck lobby, out of the sight of the visitors who were now pouring onboard for the Drum ceremony. The Officer of the Watch, a Lieutenant Commander on this special day was waiting and the Commander was hanging around within earshot. The Leading Signalman was first to be ordered to doff his cap. When anyone is taken before an officer and is being charged with a crime the first order is to take off your cap. Then the charging person, in this case the Master at Arms reads out what crime or misdemeanour you have supposedly committed. In this case we were being charged with negligent performance of duty in that we did etc., etc.

Kettler had started to explain when there was a commotion at the entrance door to the lobby and in came the Captain looking red and embarrassed as a rather stalwart lady was in the middle of a verbal tirade. He called a halt to the proceedings and ordered us to wait in the flat adjacent to the lobby. We waited for what seemed an age then the Officer of the Watch came in and spoke to the Master at Arms. He then told us the case was dismissed and with a tremendous feeling of relief I headed back to the flag deck. Kettler seemed more disappointed than relieved so I asked him why. He said he had been waiting to get the stupid gunner for a long time and when the story was told he knew who would carry the can and it wouldn't be him.

The reason for our dismissal was the very vocal protest of the "Ladies of Devon" who through their delegate had made it quite clear that, if that poor boy was punished for failing to perform what was obviously an impossible task, the whole ceremony should be cancelled. With a couple of Admirals present and numerous newspaper reporters, the Captain had little choice but to agree to drop any charges. Of course the story went round the ship and I had to face ribald remarks such as "Call out the Marines", "Watch out for the ensign", etc., etc. As I have said, my duties were on the flag deck immediately under the bridge where the Captain was located during the time at sea.

A few days later when we were at sea he looked over the bridge to the flag deck and called, "Signalman". I stopped what I was doing and looked up saying, "Yes sir". He said, "Aren't you the one who dropped the ensign". I admitted I was. He then asked me my name and I told him. "Ah," he said, "I must remember that". To me this sounded very ominous and in view of what followed during my stay in the Devonshire I am pleased his memory wasn't all that good.

We arrived in the Mediterranean in June 1936. Shortly after we anchored in Grand Harbour Malta the first news arrived of trouble in Morocco. It became obvious that this was no local incident but a well planned uprising that soon engulfed Spain. It wasn't long before the rest of the world became involved in a variety of ways. Some picked sides and supported the side of their choice with arms and men. Others tried to stay neutral on an official basis but were greatly hampered by the activities of political organisations within their own country who insisted on getting involved These had to be policed by their own nations to stop the conflict from spreading.

As the war wore on and different parts of the country fell to one side or the other it became difficult to know who was in charge of what in order to negotiate the fate of refugees. The Devonshire had been ordered to take part in carrying out the NYON agreement. This agreement, among other things, required full protection being given to citizens of non-combatant nations who had signed the agreement. It also required that this protection be extended to ships sailing under those nations' flags. This latter became a problem for two reasons.

The first was that the Spaniards had announced an embargo against certain ports prohibiting anyone from landing food or any kind of supplies. They attempted to enforce this with the battleship "Canarias", and sundry other warships. British merchant ships were constantly trying to run through to different ports to off load food and other goods. A Spanish war ship would arrest them and they would call for help. The nearest naval ship usually British would have to go and try to extricate them. The Spaniards, quite rightly, insisted that they be taken into a Spanish port under arrest. The Navy had then to put on it's "National" hat and insist the ship be released.

This situation led to many confrontations and delicate negotiations and it was incredible that an angry shot was never fired by the British. The closest it ever came was when the battleship Canarias ordered a British cruise ship with all its passengers to accompany it to the nearest Spanish port. A British destroyer was just over the horizon and arrived within an hour. The destroyer took up position between the liner and the battleship at a distance of about one mile. The Canarias trained all her guns on the destroyer, ordered her to leave the area and threatened to open fire unless her order was obeyed. The destroyer indicated she must regretfully decline and went on to point out that this was a British ship.

The Canarias stated that some of the passengers were Spanish citizens who were wanted by the authorities in Spain. She then repeated the threat with a time limit within which it must be obeyed. The destroyer again regretfully declined and pointed out that she had eight torpedoes and at a distance of one mile she would be most surprised and in fact annoyed if any of them missed. The Canarias decided that in this instance she would make an exception and let the ship go. The destroyer escorted the liner out of harms way.

The German navy was not so forgiving. For some violation of German citizen's rights the battleship Deutschland stood off and bombarded Algeciras. The bombardment went on for a considerable time and the Spaniards suffered many casualties.

As time wore on the situation became increasingly difficult to control. Some ships were becoming well known blockade runners and constantly had to be rescued.

One particular ship was constantly in trouble. The Captain had been nicknamed "Potato Jones", due to his constant running of the blockade with food supplies, particularly potatoes. It was obvious that he was being backed by either politically motivated groups or a group of do-gooders who, like so many of these groups did not realise the lives they were putting at risk or who didn't care as long as they themselves were not at risk. In addition it became obvious that food was not the only thing being carried by these blockade-runners.

The supply of arms and even men volunteers from other nations were being smuggled into Spain. As the opposing armies fought and as each city fell to one side or another the problem of non combatants caught in the middle of some of the most brutal fighting ever seen became the focus of nations who had signed the NYON agreement. It had been agreed that all refugees irrespective of nationality except Spanish nationals were to be rescued and removed from Spain.

To the Devonshire, who had anticipated only British refugees, this meant that we must be prepared to accept a far greater number than the present plans had considered. Madrid was almost certain to fall within a few days and the concentration of British subjects alone in that city was high. When all other nationalities were added, the numbers exceeded the capacity of the ships available. The nearest port for the Devonshire was Valencia, so this became our destination. Messages from distraught relatives in Britain were forwarded by the Admiralty to the Devonshire giving details of their missing families.

One such message was from Randolph Churchill, son of Winston Churchill who requested that all efforts be made to locate and give passage to Clare Luce the actress and all expenses incurred should be billed to him. When we arrived off Valencia we were instructed to lay outside the three mile limit. Apparently the Spanish were going to make things as difficult as they could. The Gunnery officer, (a young Lieutenant) was put in charge of a landing party of eight men plus one signalman.

Being the most junior onboard, I was still classed as a boy signalman; I was detailed to go with the landing party. I carried an Aldis Lamp and a signal pad. I couldn't see them doing me much good if the natives were hostile. None of the landing party were armed, an omission I thought was rather foolhardy. This was apparently in accordance with protocol. You cannot land armed men in a 'friendly' country. We arrived at the jetty, which turned out to be an enormous span of concrete as big as half a football field. This was totally surrounded on the landside by a fence about twelve feet high with double gates. This was a disembarkation point for heavy goods that had to be inspected before being allowed in to the country. It was certainly perfect for our purpose. We were watched as we disembarked by groups of people outside the fence. There were men, women and children and somehow they conveyed an atmosphere of despair. There was none of the calling and curiosity of the children who seemed to cling in fear to the adults. The men seemed to be looking anywhere except straight at us.

It became obvious that these people were living in terrible fear and wanted to avoid contact with anyone in case they became involved in something that caused more problems. It was a depressing and heart breaking sight that was unfortunately repeated many times during our tour of duty. We hadn't been on the jetty for five minutes when a contingent of Spanish consular and other authorities arrived in a huge Mercedes. One of them was a very small fat man dressed in a uniform that looked as if it was made from gold braid with odd pieces of dark material sewn in to hold it together. Everyone spoke English, even the uniformed man, although his English was hesitant compared with the fluency of the others.

They had a meeting with the Gunnery officer and it became a very heated exchange with much pointing at the men and the ship. Finally the Gunnery officer came over to where we were standing and called me to him. "Make a signal to the ship" and he dictated it, "I have been ordered by Spanish authorities to return to the ship with all hands except the signalman. Permission will be granted for a landing party to process refugees when sufficient numbers arrive. Request instructions." As I transmitted the message it's full impact dawned on me. I was going to be left here on my own surrounded by, what looked like, a gang of armed bandits.

The reply came from the ship. In it they requested the permission of the Spanish authorities to send ashore supplies that would be necessary for the processing of refugees. Again there was much argument and finally the small man in uniform agreed as long as the supplies were landed and left until refugees arrived. The Gunnery officer and landing party left in the launch. Before they left the Gunnery officer assured me that they would be back shortly with supplies and he believed that sufficient refugees would have arrived making it possible for the landing party to stay. I asked one of the landing party to bring me back a carton of cigarettes as I had been constantly asked for cigarettes as I had none left. He gave me his packet and promised to bring a carton on the return journey.

The raggle taggle group that seemed to represent the army stood around the compound talking and smoking. They were armed with a variety of weapons from shot guns to the type known in those days as "Tommy" guns as used by Chicago gangsters during Prohibition. Their age varied from what I judged to be about twelve to grey haired men. The twelve year old juggled what looked like a service revolver in his hand and constantly tried to twirl it around. I made sure I never got anywhere near the front of him and I was lucky I didn't. On one of his efforts he almost dropped the gun, grabbed at it and it fired. The bullet hit the concrete and whined over the head of one of the men who promptly went over, smacked him on the head and took away the gun.

This incident did nothing to calm my nerves. The waiting seemed endless, the sun was getting very hot as it approached noon. The concrete reflected the glare and soon the Spaniards withdrew from the quay and took shelter in the shadow of a nearby warehouse. The "Admiral", as I had mentally dubbed him, withdrew outside the fence with his two shotgun carrying guards but not before he had asked me for cigarettes. I gave him half the packet I was left with, and he was all smiles. The boat returned and unloaded a trestle table, a cardboard carton containing documents, three large boxes containing sandwiches and three barricoes of fresh water complete with tin cups. The sailors stood the barricoes at one end of the table and I was the first to use one. The "Admiral" entered the game again and insisted the landing party take off until the refugees arrived. The Gunnery officer was furious but he could do nothing about it and with extremely bad grace returned to the launch.

I had received the carton of cigarettes and under the envious eyes of the "Admiral" I tore it open and extracted a pack. I handed it to him and his face was wreathed in smiles. I gave him two more packs and simply waved at the other Spaniards who were standing around. He walked around like some self-important bishop bestowing a benediction as he gave a cigarette to each of the motley throng. They all then withdrew into the shadows outside the fence leaving me in the blazing sun. The only shade was that cast by the table so I went and sat under it. In the distance I could see the ship and it seemed to shimmer as the evaporated moisture rose from the sea. It was deadly quiet and I dozed fitfully against one leg of the table.

The silence was shattered by the sound of a bus engine that roared as if it would tear itself out of its mountings. A huge bus in an advanced state of dilapidation pulled up at the gates and a truly mixed throng started to emerge as if they could not get out fast enough. I emerged from under the table and a shout went up, "Look, look the Navy", then a ragged cheer. There are some moments in my chequered career that stand out vividly; this was one of those moments. People were cheering at the sight of a seventeen year old, strictly on his own, his only claim to fame being his Royal Navy uniform. I went over to the gate where the Spaniards were preventing people from entering the compound.

The "Admiral" was busy bouncing around issuing orders and I could see him preening himself as he passed a group of young women. As I approached I heard him calling out, "Passports, show all your passports". The people simply crowded around the gate and to all intents and purposes ignored him as they called out questions to me. He was furious. I raised both hands in the air and within seconds there was silence with those at the front telling the one's at the back to "shut up".

I asked the people in front to pass the word to queue up four deep round the fence. This was passed around quickly and I heard the people in front shouting, "The Navy wants us to queue", I had turned from a boy signalman into the whole Navy, it felt good. I started to do a rough count and then stopped. A whole line of these buses was entering the dock area, stopping, then pouring forth dozens more refugees. The buses were obviously overloaded and carrying far more passengers than they were designed to carry. I counted seven more buses, which meant at least four hundred people.

This exodus proved to be people brought most of the way by train from Madrid. Later I saw movies and read stories about the last train from Madrid. None of the stories, and certainly the movie, came anywhere near the reality of that moment. I knew I had to get on the Aldis lamp and inform the ship. I didn't know what to do to keep the crowd from breaking in the gates, which they showed every sign of doing despite the "Admiral" and his bodyguard.

I talked to the people at the head of the queue and asked them to pass the word that I was telling the ship of their arrival and please be patient. They did and the effect was magical. They settled down to wait. I called the ship with the terse message, "Refugees arrived." I was immediately asked, "How many?" I replied that there seemed to be around four hundred. I had to repeat that figure twice before they accepted it. I asked for instructions and I was told to wait until the ship sent out a launch with a support party. I looked around, the people were waiting patiently outside the gates and the "Admiral" was walking up and down in front of the queue like a model at a fashion show. I suggested to him that by opening the gates we could get the people through in an orderly fashion and examine their passports as they passed through the gate in single file.

I called him "Sir" constantly and refilled his cigarette supply on a regular basis. I pointed out that there were a large number of people, the sun was very hot and if they felt nothing was happening they could become very angry. He eventually agreed and the people passed through and for the most part they sat on the concrete in orderly lines. This move seemed to relieve the tension as they felt something was happening. They seemed to think that inside the fence was somehow Royal Navy territory.

There were citizens of almost every non-combatant country but mostly British. A large number were troupes of girls from dance theatres touring Spain from Britain. There were several well-known actors and a few prominent British citizens but Claire Luce was not among them. It was blazingly hot and everyone was trying to shade themselves under newspaper hats or anything else that came in handy. Some had just one bag but there were several who had somehow managed to travel with several cases. The "Admiral" was constantly making a nuisance of himself asking totally irrelevant questions and practising his English on what he thought were the best looking of the girls. I thought they were all good looking. One of them asked me if there was any water available and I suddenly felt stupid.

There were barricoes of water and boxes of sandwiches I had forgotten about. I realised that if I made an announcement there would be a terrible rush. I called a man over who had been pointed out to me as a travel guide. I asked him if he could speak several languages. Enough to get by he answered so I asked him to tell everyone to stay in their place and volunteers would bring round water and food. The cheer that went up was good to hear. I asked several men and women to take cups of water round. Fortunately the ship had provided a whole case of thick navy mugs so distribution was no problem. When the sandwich boxes were opened they contained thick slices of bread with tinned corned beef in between.

It was a sight to behold. The people ate them as if they were the finest food they had ever seen. I had tremendous difficulty with the "Admiral" who wanted to serve out sandwiches to his band of supporters who were crowding round outside the fence. It took a lot of persuasion for him to finally concede that this would not be right but not before he heard the growls of anger coming from the crowd and the sight of half a dozen rather large men who, seeing my problem came and stood behind me without saying a word. They were wonderful people, men, women and lots of children who, once I had told them that the ship was sending boats for them, settled in and never pestered me with questions I could not answer, such as, "How long will it be", "Where will we be taken" etc., etc.

It was almost three hours after my message that the first of the boats from the ship arrived. The delay had been caused by trying to arrange and rig up sleeping accommodation together with the necessity of feeding such a number for an extended period. It was almost sunset before the last boat was ready to depart. One of the young ladies asked if this was the last boat and was she the last passenger. When she was told she was, she went back up steps to where the "Admiral" was standing near the edge of the jetty. He grinned all over his stupid face when she approached him. He had singled her out and had been making offensive remarks to her all day. I think he thought she was going to wish him a special goodbye. She did. With one push she pushed him off the jetty into the water. She ran back to the boat and the Coxswain needed no urging to take off. We watched as he splashed and floundered his way to the steps to be helped by his bodyguard. There was an official protest but by the time it reached us we were in Marseilles disembarking refugees after a miserable crossing in rough weather. The cramped accommodation, the limitation of food (mostly bacon and beans), and the violent seasickness made them all glad to get off the ship.

After we had discharged the refugees in Marseilles we were ordered to Palma Majorca and Ibiza where it was understood that several British people wanted to be taken onboard. The clean up necessary after the refugees was a full time job that was undertaken by the Stokers and the Seamen of the duty watch. This led to an enormous amount of grumbling because the stokers had also been pressed into service serving meals to the trestle tables set up for the refugees and had been subjected to a great deal of criticism and abuse over the quality and quantity of the meals.

This criticism had been so bad coming from a clique that had been formed at the end of one table that a two-badge stoker, (a man with long service) dumped a basin of hot mashed potatoes over the head of the leader of the clique. Then challenged the others collectively to get on their feet so he could knock them down. This was accompanied by cheers from the adjacent refugees who obviously were fed up with these people. The men challenged decided not to accept the challenge particularly since a half a dozen other stokers had mysteriously appeared alongside the first stoker. He was placed in the Commanders report and was awaiting his judgement. When it arrived it was one day's stoppage of leave effective immediately. In the middle of the Mediterranean it would be rather remarkable if anyone could get ashore, so the punishment fit the crime.

We arrived in the harbour at Palma and sent a landing party ashore. Naturally I was with them but, this time there were no untoward incidents and the British Consul informed the Captain that anyone wanting to leave had already left We returned to the ship and hardly arrived onboard when an air raid started. Bombs were dropped near the Cathedral and one in the harbour. Nothing came near us but for the first time I felt that nervous tingling, anticipation of the sky about to fall, a feeling I have felt more times than I can remember now but it is one the human body can never get used to.

Apparently the ship had been informed about some British Citizens being held in Ibiza against their will. We arrived off Ibiza and it was here I once again distinguished myself with an ensign. As we approached the harbour we could see that the Spanish ensign had been replaced by the new rebel ensign. We were carrying both ensigns at the mainmast because protocol demanded that when entering a port we had to fly the appropriate ensign and fire the correct salute from the saluting guns. Both ensigns were very similar in colour, particularly when rolled up. I was sent aft to hoist the ensign and when it hit the block the first gun was fired. Naturally they were blanks but they made an awful noise. As we approached a launch full of dignitaries had headed out to meet us but on the first round the boat turned and went full out for the shore.

The guns continued their salute and all eyes were on the rapidly receding boat, fortunately. I looked up and saw that I had hoisted the wrong ensign. It took me a few frantic seconds to haul it down and hoist the rebel ensign, which was already fastened to another pair of halyards. Incredibly no one noticed and I left it flying and returned to the flag deck. The protest that followed was a half hearted one as the people in the boat admitted that the similarity in colour and the distance combined with the unexpected gunfire had confused the coxswain of their boat.

There was a large army contingent on the island and the non commissioned officers had mutinied and taken over the very large barracks. We watched through binoculars as some of the officers were placed before a wall and shot. Our Commander accompanied by a very large armed able seaman as a bodyguard went ashore. Our launch stood off ready to bring him off and I was the signalman in the launch. My orders from the Commander were to signal the ship the moment he arrived back onboard. It was a very tense waiting period of almost two hours.

The Commander arrived back walking down the jetty as if he was strolling in the park. An elderly, heavily sunburned man accompanied him. It turned out that this man had been on the island for many years and had been reluctant to leave with the others. He had finally been arrested by the Sergeant who was now the Commanding Officer of the local garrison. I was told that our Commander had difficulty persuading the Sergeant to release the man. Finally he told him that if the man and himself were not in the boat within half an hour the ship would open fire on the barracks. Whether this is true or not I cannot say but they certainly hurried them down to the boat.

The ship continued its duty of patrolling for the next several months with occasional bursts of excitement that turned out to be insignificant. The war raged on and there was little that could be done other than evacuating refugees and trying to prevent ships running the gauntlet to sell their cargo to the highest bidder.

CHAPTER FOUR

Chain of Command

In the Devonshire, for the first time I began to be able to assess fully the Navy and the people around me. The ship's company was a closely-knit community, particularly those who were members of the same branch. The length of service of the men varied from less than two years to more than twenty. We had Able Seamen with nothing but three badges showing their length of service to be beyond 12 years to a variety of Chief and Petty Officers the youngest being about 35 years of age. Some were wearing the medals of World War One together with a variety of medals awarded in campaigns about which I had never heard.

Time passed extraordinarily quickly as every day was full of duties to be performed and when off watch, the hundred and one things necessary to keep clean in clothes and body. There was never a shortage of things to do from playing "Tombola"; civilians call it Bingo to putting together a concert party to entertain each other.

We were able to have shore leave in all the ports of the Mediterranean but the base was Malta and when alongside or at anchor we took full advantage of the sights, sounds and smells. Malta was known to us as the island of "Smells, Bells and dirty Gels". An unfortunate reputation but in those days I think it was well earned. It is quite true that with the wind blowing in the right direction when you were several miles out at sea the island gave off a peculiar earthy smell and as for the bells, there seemed to be hundred of church steeples each containing one or more bells. On Sunday and on religious holidays the bells started early in the morning and the cacophony went on all day. As for the "Gels", there was an area of downtown Valleta known as "The Gut". It was a steep street partly stepped with dance halls, bars and casinos lining both sides. The girls in very abbreviated dress would stand at the entrance to their particular place and implore the sailors to come in. Naturally many of the sailors succumbed, without much protest, to their entreaties and when the fleet was in the whole of Valletta and in particular "The Gut" was a hive of activity.

Fortunately, I being a boy and then an ordinary signalman at this period had neither the amount of shore leave nor the money to indulge in these pleasures or I undoubtedly would have done. It was a wonderful learning experience however that stayed with me all my life. The lessons I learned from those who did indulge was sufficient to make me very circumspect in my shore activities.

Being in the Signal Branch meant that my watches were kept on the Flag Deck or the Bridge. I was therefore at an early age exposed to officers to an extent that was far greater than other members of the ship's company. This situation continued throughout my time in the service as subsequent chapters will tell. I had no background to prepare me on what to expect so every encounter and observation of this then, privileged class , made an impact.

One of the first things I realised was that the officers treated the Navy as if it was their own private yacht club. In addition to the necessary diplomatic parties when arriving at a port there was a constant floating cocktail party whenever we were alongside. This would not have been hard to put up with if they had done their own preparation and left the ship's company alone. Instead, they used everyone from the wardroom cooks and stewards to the duty watch to rig awnings, run boats to ships at anchor to bring guests and generally treat the sailors as family retainers.

It was inevitable in the running daily routine of ship that messages would arrive and be required to be delivered to officers in the middle of these parties. This meant that whoever was delivering the messages had to be turned out in his best uniform and unfortunately as the junior member this duty fell to me on many occasions. To say I resented it was to put it too mildly; I hated it. I hated the condescension on the face of the officers to whom the message was being delivered. They would be having an animated discussion with some female trying to impress her with their importance. As I approached they would wave me to a standstill and continue talking for a while as if I didn't exist. Sometimes they would turn with a start as if they had forgotten my existence. Other times the lady to whom he was talking would interrupt him by nodding in my direction. This would make him snap at me as if I was responsible for the interruption.

Most of the messages were simply routine, but they gave the officer a chance to show his importance and devotion to duty. I remember on one occasion when the message informed us that the "Gash" boat (service name for the garbage collecting boat) would be alongside the following day. I took it to the duty officer, a young lieutenant, who promptly excused himself from his female companion after frowning over the message, "This is a little urgent," he said and hurried me away. He told me to give it to the Chief Boatswain's mate while he lingered behind a turret to impress the lady with his importance and devotion to duty. It made me sick to see this posturing and artificial pretence.

Unfortunately this attitude was the normal rather than the exception. Some of the officers came from distinguished and aristocratic families and, strangely enough they were the most approachable and likeable of them all. They treated everyone with courtesy and they gave absolute recognition to the fact that the ship's company, particularly the Chiefs and Petty Officers were professionals and actually ran the ship. Most of the others tried to carry out some kind of an imitation of what they thought a gentleman should be and they failed miserably. Even their speech was false, for, when they were in the company of senior officers or entertaining ladies they spoke with a peculiar high pitch that sounded like a constant "Haw Haw" and they pronounced their words as if they had a ball in their mouth.

For the first time in my life I had come across snobbery and I did not like it. There were many examples of it, and, thinking that we were ignorant of their foibles they were quite open about it in our presence. We would occasionally carry for working experience, officers from the Merchant Navy who were also classed as Royal Navy Reserve and served in royal fleet auxiliaries. These men had come up the hard way, were extremely competent seamen but were not the product of Naval Colleges. They still retained their original dialect that could be anywhere from English spoken with a broad Scots accent or Yorkshire or Lancashire men to the Welsh of very "Welsh Wales".

These officers would be on the bridge and stand watch with the Officer of the Watch. When their back was turned the other officers would go into an imitation of their dialect and introduce comments into their speech such as "EE Bar Gum Lad" and "What yer up to Scouse". They forgot that we who were listening, had the same dialects and this built up a deep contempt for the officers involved and unfortunately officers in general. This feeling persisted with all of us with the result that all officers were regarded in a very poor light until they proved otherwise, which, thank heaven, a great many did.

The relationship between officers and men in the Navy is a delicate one more than in the other armed forces. Except for navigation and ship handling the expertise rested in the hands of the ship's company particularly the Chief and Petty Officers, with two exceptions on a large ship. These were the Engineer Officer and the Doctor. Every part of the ship had an officer in charge that was theoretically responsible for it's efficiency. Under him was a Chief or Petty Officer who was in practice responsible. The system for the most part worked well. The theory was that if anything went wrong the Officer in charge was responsible. However this was just a theory and led to many foul ups, some of a dangerous nature. One incident arose when we were going to anchor in a fairway outside a port in the Mediterranean. The officer in charge of the forecastle told the Petty Officer that they were going to anchor using the port anchor. The Petty Officer told him that there was an inadequate length of cable on the port anchor for the depth of water.

He told him they had been working in the cable locker that day and the starboard anchor had adequate cable and was secured in the locker. How many shackles of cable are there on the port anchor he was asked, to which he replied Six Shackles. "I consider that will be enough "said the officer. But it is not secured he was told and he replied there would be enough left inboard. The Petty Officer could not believe his ears and persisted with his objections and here the system falls over. He was told to obey the order at once. He now had a choice. He could refuse to carry out the order, in which case he would be severely punished or he could inform the Captain.

I was the Flag boy, that is I held up the flag for the number of shackles that were let out when they stopped and also held up the flag that told the bridge the anchor cable was straight up and down when retrieving the anchor. I heard the verbal exchange and to this day, in all fairness, I do not think the Officer heard the words that the anchor cable was not secured. He was making his decision on the six shackles. I definitely heard the words but no one ever asked for my contribution, naturally.

The Petty Officer could take the risk of informing the Captain of his doubts and no matter which way the issue was resolved his career would be finished. The officers stood by each other whether right or wrong He could go ahead and accept the fallacy that the Fo'c'sle Officer would be held responsible. He decided to go ahead. The order came from the bridge to let go anchor. Normally the Leading Seaman would wield the sledgehammer that released the anchor but the Petty Officer ordered him and everyone to stand well clear. He then released the anchor with a single blow and as the anchor dropped pulling the heavy cable out of the locker the Petty Officer ran to the aft of the forecastle with the others. The cable came roaring out of the locker then the end of it appeared and lashed across the forecastle before vanishing into the water. Anyone standing in their normal positions would have been killed.

There was a roar from the bridge to drop a buoy to mark the anchor position. This would normally have taken some time to do but unknown to the Forecastle Officer, the Petty Officer had a buoy rigged and ready and immediately the order came the buoy was dropped. They were then told to drop the starboard anchor, which was carried out successfully. The problem now was to recover the anchor and the cable attached to the anchor. The diving boat was lowered and the two divers together with the shipwright, with all their gear, two Able Seamen, a Signalman, me, and the officer designated as diving officer.

Two seamen rowed the boat back towards the buoy as the divers prepared. In those days the divers went down in complete suits with lead boots and a helmet through which the air was pumped. There had to be two fully rigged divers in case of difficulties. The boat was secured to the buoy line and the one of the divers prepared to go over the side. The seamen were now manning the pump on the compressor which would send the air to the divers.

They had brought with them a coil of flexible steel cable and the concept was for the diver to take it down to the anchor, secure the end and then secure the boat end of the cable to a shackle fixed in the boat. This was carried out smoothly and efficiently. We let go of the buoy and now we were being held in position by the cable attached to the anchor. The ship would then come alongside and lower a cable to hoist the anchor inboard. We had a huge crane onboard and we anticipated this would be used for the task.

The Diving officer told me to signal to the ship that we were ready, which I did. The ship got underway and moved towards us. As the wind was blowing in our direction from the ship we anticipated the ship would come up on our port side so that the wind would be in our favour and hold us alongside. To our horror the ship came to us on our starboard side and the wind steadily pushed the ship against us until the boat, held by the cable started to tilt. The divers were frantically trying to get out of their lead boots and suit otherwise they would sink like stones. The shipwright was desperately trying to release the inboard end of the cable with no success, as it was by now bar taut. The water was now beginning to pour over the gunwales and a diver, giving up hope of getting undressed in time, swung an axe at the cable where it went over the gunwale. He must have carved away a foot of the gunwale before a blow severed the last strands of the cable and the boat righted itself. We were standing waist deep in water.

The ship had been oblivious to our fate as we were under the bows where we could not be seen. I was fully prepared to swim for my life. We pulled clear of the ship, went round in a circle and came alongside the gangway. It wasn't until then that the Captain became aware of what had happened. There was a Court of Enquiry in which of course I took no part except to testify that we were indeed in danger of sinking. This was already known from the other witnesses but they have to always slam the stable doors. It was at this court of enquiry that the circumstances leading up to the loss of the anchor was revealed.

Where did the responsibility lie? Obviously the rules were that the officer in charge was responsible and in this case it was so clear-cut, so we thought. Not so, the Petty Officer was punished, as he did not make abundantly clear to the Officer that the cable was not shackled in the cable locker. He said at the enquiry that he had specifically informed the Officer that the cable was not secured. The Officer denied this and despite The Leading Seaman's testimony and a description of the Petty Officers action to avoid injury on the forecastle, they believed the Officer. In view of this finding the Officer was cleared. It was as a result of this that my assessment of officers ever after was done very carefully

The term "Officers and Gentlemen" vanished from my vocabulary. Every one I have ever served with has been viewed with a jaundiced eye until I became familiar with them. I have met many fine officers with whom it has been a privilege to serve. I have also met walking disasters but fortunately they have been in the minority.

The normal term for a ship to carry out a foreign commission in those days was two and a half years. This was particularly hard on those of the ship's company who were married. It wasn't too bad for the officers as those that were married could usually afford to bring their wives out to Malta or to different ports of call. The children were of course no problem for, as was customary in their class, they were in boarding schools. For the men of course these expensive habits were out of the question and they and their wives were resigned to the long absences.

CHAPTER FIVE

Going Home

It came as a wonderful surprise and the news was greeted with cheers when in early 1937 were told that we would be returning to the U.K for the Coronation of George VI. The fleet were to be in review at Spithead in the month of May to celebrate this auspicious occasion. We left Malta in late April for the journey home. It is difficult to describe the feeling of elation that pervaded the ship. Everyone was on his very best behaviour in case something happened to prevent his trip home.

The sprucing up and cleaning and painting went on ceaselessly. Paintwork shone. Brasswork gleamed and the woodwork was sanded to a golden sheen. The atmosphere on the ship was such that the First Lieutenant (Jimmy the One), as he is called, arranged extra make and mends to give everyone a chance to spruce up his personal kit. The term "make and mend " is lost in the history of the Royal Navy. It was in use before Nelson's time and is used to indicate that for a specified period of time the ship's company can attend to their personal needs. In the old days this was essential as the men did make and mend their own clothes, in modern times it is used to grant shore leave and permit other leisure activities.

The journey back passed very quickly and I am certain that once alongside the ship was inspected by every Admiral that existed, or so it seemed. These inspections were something that had to be seen to be believed. Despite the fact that hundreds of men ate, slept and had their full lives to live in a confined space, a pretence existed that there were no such things as "Gash" buckets (garbage bins), Used cooking utensils, these had to be polished to a brilliant shine. Hammocks that appeared slightly worn had to hidden at the bottom of the hammock rack and wooden mess tables that had to be "shark skinned "until they were white.

The Admiral and his retinue would arrive onboard and, followed by an anxious Captain and ship's officers would tour every part of the ship. In every inspection I saw there was one sycophant, usually a Commander with the party who wore white gloves. He would run his hand on the overhead steel beams and behind lockers in places where, unless you were a contortionist you couldn't possibly get at to clean. He would then wave his hand, which was obviously dusty towards the Admiral for him to see. I often wondered when they left the ship if the Admiral patted him on the head and said, “Good boy.”

They would demand to see a list of the ship’s stores and point to an obscure item and tell the supply people to produce it and time them to see how fast they could produce the item. On one occasion they selected an item called a “Shove Wood”. By it’s name it appeared to be something that would be used to load wood on the lumber rack which every ship had. The ship’s Supply Officer turned to the able seaman messenger and sent him to the stores department to tell the stores man to bring the “Shove Wood”. While the messenger was away there was some discussion with the Supply Officer as to why a cruiser would carry such an item that, according to the Admiral, he had never come across before.

The Supply Officer went into a detailed description of what it was and how it was used and he certainly had a vivid imagination. The Supply Petty Officer arrived on the scene looking somewhat confused. “Where is the shove wood?” demanded the Supply Officer. The Petty Officer looked at him and asked if he could see the book. It was handed over with a finger pointing at the offending item. “Oh that” he said, “That is a misprint, it should read “Wood Shovel, 1 in number. See the asterisk at the bottom of the page with the correct wording”.

There was a deadly hush and the Supply Officers face went scarlet. Nothing more was said and the inspection team went on its way. Afterwards, for a long time, whenever he was in earshot of men working, you would hear one of them ask another to pass the “Shove Wood”. I do not know what the reaction of the Admiral was afterwards but I certainly would not have liked to be in the Supply Officer’s shoes.

These inspections severely disrupted everyday life. In fact they made it miserable. Can you imagine a working party moving well ahead of the inspection team carrying garbage buckets, cleaning materials and other essentials for daily life so that the Admiral would not see them and could pretend that no such thing existed? We couldn’t even go to the “Heads” (toilets) while the inspection team was doing their rounds.

The great day came and it was a glorious sight with ships lying in perfect lines as far as the eye could see. The Royal Yacht “Britannia “moved through the columns to the accompaniment of piped salutes from each ship followed by the usual three cheers. The weather was kind and the masses of small boats with their passengers sailed past, barely missing being run down but with the people standing up recklessly and cheering. It was on this type of rare occasion that I felt that what I was doing was worthwhile but I repeat, it was rare.

During our short stay in Devonport, we were given 7 days leave. A most unexpected bonus for a ship's company that had not expected to see their families for two and a half years. We had the usual round of visitors and the officers their cocktail parties and then we were headed back to Malta to complete our commission. We did the usual exercises on the way back, with gunnery practice almost every day although we actually fired the guns quite rarely. The practice consisted of going to action stations, loading and unloading and bringing up ammunition from the magazines. Every thing was timed so that there was constant competition between one guns crew and another. On the bridge we took part in flag hoisting exercises with the Chief Yeoman shouting out the signal and signalman on each side competing to beat each other to be first to get them to the yardarm.

We arrived back in Malta, much to the delight of the local population. The Royal Navy in those days provided most of the money flowing into the island. The fleet was anchored in Grand Harbour and here, in addition to being under the scrutiny of the Admiral in charge of the Cruiser squadron; we had the battleship Queen Elizabeth with the Admiral in charge of the Mediterranean fleet onboard. The Flag Lieutenant to the Admiral was Lord Louis Mountbatten, who was I think, a Lieut. Commander at the time. He took his duties very seriously for in his position he was also the Fleet Signal Officer.

He introduced the idea of making a message on the masthead light anytime during the night without warning. The message would contain a question on almost any subject and the signalman on watch would have to find the answer and when asked had to give it on a light that could only be read by the Queen Elizabeth. Had he confined his questions to the field of communications it would have been at least reasonable but he didn't. His questions ranged from asking the height of Mount Everest to subjects from the Guinness Book of Records. A message would be sent to the ships the following morning giving their standing from the night before. Needless to say the Captains of the ships wanted to be first and many a Chief Yeoman spent a sleepless night trying to back up his staff, his who also suffered.

When you have been at sea keeping constant watches your in harbour time is precious and the number on watch would be reduced to the minimum. With this exercise we had to keep a full complement on watch so that they could carry out research and still keep an eye on the fleet. I am afraid he wasn't very popular.

At eight in the morning a message would be sent by radio Morse to all ships present giving the dress of the day and whatever other instructions the Admiral wanted to convey. The message was broadcast on one frequency and replied to on another. Lord Louis had the mistaken impression that he could transmit and read as fast as the ship's radio operators and used to go to the radio room and transmit the long morning message himself.

The operators in the fleet knew immediately when he was on the circuit and the time taken would be many times longer than a trained operator could transmit. Naturally nobody could say anything but one morning he was worse than usual. An operator came in on the other frequency and interrupted him to send a message. When Lord Louis gave him the go ahead his message was "Try using your feet". Everyone in the fleet heard it and Lord Louis demanded over the circuit that the operator identify himself. The answer was "What you don't know can't hurt me". The fleet operators all knew each other's Morse sending technique, it was very individual, but no one, when questioned could possibly identify the guilty operator. That was the last time this routine was carried out and everyone breathed easier.

CHAPTER SIX

Incompetence

I had been studying and doing fleet examinations while in the Devonshire and had successfully qualified as a full signalman and then qualified as, what was known in those days, a "Trained operator". This qualification enabled me to be the senior signalman on watch and also to stand a watch on my own if I were sent to a Destroyer. This happened almost immediately after I qualified and I found myself onboard H.M.S. Grafton, a destroyer serving with the Mediterranean fleet.

Little did I realise it but that was the beginning of my life in a navy that was the same but totally different from any other. I found that the officers were somehow a different breed and so were the men. There was an efficiency and dedication about them that I had never experienced before. On the bridge the signalman was treated as an individual who knew his job and was listened to when manoeuvres were being carried out and was assisted by anyone standing by when receiving a message. He would read the message and the nearest person would grab a signal pad and write it down as he spoke it aloud. It was not unusual for the Officer of the Watch to do this and on several occasions the Captain would help out. We only had four Signalmen and a Yeoman so we all had to carry our weight with only one to a watch.

We spent a great deal of time at sea. No large ship could go out on exercises without destroyers forming a screen around her as would happen in war to provide protection against submarine attack. This type of exercise was very regular. Then there were exercises which only destroyers would carry out, torpedo attacks, target shooting at floating targets and drones towed by aircraft and submarine hunting. I enjoyed this. The officers were dedicated and efficient professionals and the ship's company had a total familiarity with their jobs that made life so much more pleasant than the artificial world of the large ship.

We obviously had to have the occasional hiccup when a man would be drafted to the ship and turn out to be incompetent or a constant moaner. Unfortunately the large ships had a tendency to get rid of this type of person and would send them anywhere to get them off of the ship. With such a small crew living in terribly confined space someone like this wreaked havoc on the morale. They never lasted very long and it was better to sail short handed than put up with this type of disruption.

It was, however, quite rare to have an officer arrive as a replacement who could not fully pull his weight as every one of them had to be fully qualified watch keeping officers with some experience. This was understandable as, contrary to large ship practice, there was only one officer on the bridge at a time so he had to know his way around. Unfortunately one of our watch keeping officers was taken ill with appendicitis and a rapid replacement had to be borrowed from a battleship in the harbour to fill in while he was away.

They sent us a newly commissioned Warrant Officer who had just received his watch keeping certificate onboard the battleship Queen Elizabeth. Different to the Army, a Warrant Officer in the Navy is a fully commissioned officer who has been promoted from the lower deck. They were normally referred to as Boatswains (Bo' suns) so you would have a signal boatswain, a torpedo boatswain etc. They were never carried in destroyers unless the destroyer carried the senior officer of the destroyer flotilla.

In the two days before we left harbour for exercises it became obvious that we had a problem on our hands. Instead of falling in to the disciplined yet relaxed routine of a destroyer he made himself a pain in the neck by interfering in the work of the Chief Gunners Mate. It turned out that he had been a Gunners Mate before his promotion, and he did not seem to realise that this was a destroyer where total reliance was placed on the ship's company. We sailed on exercises and the Chief breathed a sigh of relief at getting him out of his hair.

In getting out of the Chiefs hair he was now keeping watch on the bridge where, when left on his own he conducted himself as if he was on the Admirals Bridge of a Flagship. He sent the Boatswains Mate on useless errands; he constantly upbraided the lookouts for not reporting objects that were obviously flotsam. One look out started to report sea gulls whenever one appeared and to our amusement was acknowledged by a "Very Good". We were in the company of four other destroyers and were going out on night exercises. During these, as in war, all ships are darkened and on a moonless night are extremely difficult to see.

We carried out the exercise, which finished about midnight, but the ships were ordered to stay darkened. We were the last ship in the single line and kept proper station by watching the phosphorus kicked up by the wake of the ship ahead. It wasn't easy but with diligence it was possible. I had the middle watch from 12 until 4 and found that the Officer of the Watch was the new arrival. It started to get a little chilly and he turned to me and told me to go to his cabin and bring up his gloves. I thought he did not know so I told him I was the Signalman. He retorted that he knew full well who I was and repeated the order to get his gloves. I informed him as politely as I could that the Captain's orders specifically stated that a signalman had to be on the bridge at all times.

He replied that the order really meant that someone who was capable of reading signals should be on the bridge. As he had just completed his officers' course he was fully competent to read any signals that were made. I still objected so he gave me a direct order to leave the bridge. I left the bridge and was in no hurry to return. I went to the galley and had a cup of cocoa and a cigarette. I talked about the latest news with a nearby shipmate then wandered down to his cabin, got the gloves and returned to the bridge.

He grumbled at the time I had taken but he couldn't do anything about that. It takes about twenty minutes for eyes to become fully accustomed to the dark after leaving a lighted area. I waited and watched through the binoculars but even after twenty minutes I could not detect the wake of the ship ahead. I went to the rear of the bridge and asked the "look outs" where the ship was. Both of them said they had lost sight of it and had reported the fact several minutes before. One of them said he had seen a flickering blue light just before he lost sight of the ship ahead.

I returned to the front of the bridge and reported that neither the lookouts nor I could see the ship ahead. The time was 1 a.m. and I made a note of it in my log. He pointed dead ahead and said " look carefully and you will see her, I can see her wake as plain as day". I tried, the darkness and the breaking waves play havoc with your eyes and it was conceivable that he could see the ship and I could not until I fixed in on her. I asked him about the flickering blue light and he claimed that there was no such thing.

I was becoming really worried. The routine in a fully darkened ship when a change of course was to be signalled was to flash the new course five times on a small blue light. No answer was given and none expected. The new course change was then implemented by a steady blue light that lasted about five seconds.

I felt that this must have happened and this person, despite his vaunted efficiency at being able to do everyone's job, was not even aware that such a system existed. I told him that despite my every effort I could not see the ship ahead and suggested we alert the Captain. He was furious, refused point blank and indicated that I was being insubordinate in even suggesting such a course of action. I shut up and waited.

The watch turn over came at 4 o'clock and the First Lieutenant usually stood the morning watch. My relief arrived and it was my duty to turn over everything to him such as the position of the ship relative to other ships and any signals that had been made. The First Lieutenant had taken over the watch with the verbal report that the ship ahead was maintaining her distance course and speed. It would have taken a great deal of time to wait to become accustomed to the night so at this juncture the Officer of the Watch would ask the signalman and the lookouts if they could see the ship ahead. He would then accept the watch from the outgoing officer.

I was the first one he asked and the Officer of the Watch was half way down the bridge ladder when I replied that I had not seen the ship ahead since 1 in the morning and neither had the look outs. He came storming back up the ladder saying in a furious voice that this was the last straw and he was going to charge me with insolence. The First Lieutenant intervened and said there was no problem. The Officer of the Watch however should not leave the bridge until he (The First Lieutenant) could see the ship ahead. Dawn came slowly and instead of being in my hammock I was standing on the bridge waiting for what I knew to be the truth confirmed. There was not a ship in sight and the Captain was immediately alerted. He arrived on the bridge and the First Lieutenant briefed him on the situation.

I was the first one taken to task, as I had reported not seeing the ship since 1 o'clock. I told the Captain exactly how it all happened. Of course I did not mention my trip to the galley for cocoa etc. He started to give me one terrible dressing down when the First Lieutenant coughed and intervened. He told the Captain that I had demurred until I was given a direct order. Now his wrath turned on the Officer of the Watch. He demanded an explanation then and there to the embarrassment of everyone on the bridge. It was understandable as this type of incompetence put the ship in great hazard. The explanation that he felt he could read signals as well as the Signalman was waved away and finally the Captain calmed down enough to realise that it was not quite proper to conduct an enquiry in front of everyone on the bridge.

We eventually joined up with the ships and had to endure the ribald signals about lost sheep etc. Fortunately no lasting harm was done to the ship or the Captains reputation. When we arrived back in harbour the first person over the gangway and into the boat was the Warrant Officer on his way back to his ship. We received a message asking if our missing officer had returned as they thought the Warrant Officer would be gone for much longer.

The reply sent was that in view of the known exercise future we could manage until the sick officer returned. It is impossible to keep such incidents a secret especially when it involves a very unpopular person. By all accounts he had a very hard time trying to live it down. I was given a real blast for my part in this fiasco but to this day no one has ever told me how to disobey a direct order and get away with it.

For the rest of our commission we went through all the routine of exercises; intercepted ships bound for Spanish Ports and screened the battle fleet or the aircraft carriers when they emerged from Grand Harbour. We used to say, in disparaging terms of course, that the only reason for their infrequent sea time was to move off the piles of tins they ditched over the side into the water so they wouldn't be grounded.

The trouble in Palestine erupted. I never could sort out whose side we were on or what the real issues at that time were. We and two other ships in the flotilla went there on a support mission. What we did, except be there, I have no idea. The ship I was in only stayed four days and then sailed for exercises and home. I learned much later that, every member of the ships company of the ships that were there was entitled to the Palestine Medal. We were supposed to write in and claim the medal as by the time it was awarded the ships companies were scattered far and wide. During the short time in Palestine I had been loaned to the Grenville for a few days because of sickness of one of their signalman. The whole idea struck me as being ridiculous so I never claimed the medal.

CHAPTER SEVEN

Awaiting Reassignment

In September 1938 the ship had been paid off and we were in the Barracks awaiting further drafting. The winds of war had begun to blow and ships that had been in reserve, most of them in low care and maintenance, were being reactivated. To keep us gainfully occupied I, along with a few others were sent to the Dockyard as care and maintenance crew for ships in reserve lying alongside. As we were few in number and only one ships galley was working for all the destroyers tied up alongside each other we were on canteen messing. The fact that there was no canteen seemed to have escaped the notice of the powers that be. Here I must digress to explain this peculiar anomaly.

The Navy feeds, or as their term goes, "Victuals", the ships' companies in different ways depending on the size of the ship or in some cases the circumstances surrounding a ship's situation. In cruisers and above, the term "Broadside messing" is used. In this method there is a central galley where all the cooking is done by professional cooks.

The officers have a separate galley where their food is processed. Broadside refers to the way the individual messes are laid out. Long tables normally sit broadside in the ship and, depending on the number of men in a mess the number of tables allocated can vary but it is rarely more than two. The members of the mess share an affinity, that is the stokers have a mess, the communication people have a mess and so on. The food for a mess is allocated based on numbers and the galley staff issues the food to a couple of members of the mess who take it below and share it out. Then there was, I say, was, because this system has thankfully died, Canteen messing. This was a truly botched up system where the Supply ship supplied certain basics such as meat and vegetables onboard. A money allowance was given to each man carried in a mess and from this allowance all other food was purchased. Despite

it's gross inefficiency this system persisted in the Destroyers and smaller ships until the end of the war.

It was totally inefficient because on many occasions there was no supply ship or base available and the pitifully small allowance never covered the main meal requirement from commercial outlets. We were constantly under funded and found ourselves having to subsidise out of our own pay the amount necessary to make up the difference.

Another system was known as "Cash Victualling". This was for really small ships and was exactly what it said. A fixed sum was allocated for each man onboard and they were responsible for purchasing everything they needed. In both Canteen messing and Cash victualling it was necessary for one person in the mess to co-ordinate and be responsible for the purchasing of the basics to make a meal. No one wanted the job so it was assigned on a day-to-day basis. It doesn't take much imagination to see the disasters this led to on many occasions.

We struggled along getting a ration of meat, some green vegetables, if available, and potatoes from the dockyard stores. With this we could put together a main meal at noon but for breakfast and supper we were strictly on our own. There were twelve of us scattered between the ships, one or two from each Branch. We all gathered in one mess on one of the destroyers for eating and sleeping. The situation was ridiculous and if this kind of treatment was handed out today it would make national headlines and someone would suffer, that is, if any one would believe it and I still find difficulty believing it myself.

On one occasion, it was Saturday, we had had our midday meal some hours before and now we had to think about supper. We had some corned beef in tins, some tinned sausages and that good old navy staple, tinned pilchards. None of them appealed to the majority so we had to think of something else. Here, I must digress. One of the members of the group was a signalman called Birdie Wing. In the Navy an artful dodger is known as a "Bird". This signalman both by his name and character was well named. He should have had the three Good Conduct Badges, which would normally have been awarded to him over his fifteen plus years of service. He had none; in fact it was his proud boast that he had never had one that they could take away, which was a common practice for those who often transgressed.

He was a big man, with the most devilish laughing blue eyes I had ever seen. He dressed immaculately even in our present sordid surroundings and in the tales I had heard there was not a signal staff on any ship who wouldn't welcome him. Apparently at his job he was the best. He came up with the suggestion that we should have lobsters. He knew a fishmonger, who, on Saturday, cleared out his stock of lobsters at half price. We thought it was a great idea so we all chipped in the amount he said he would need and he went. It was raining and getting dark. The rain hadn't let up all day and as he set off it seemed to get even worse.

In Devonport and Plymouth the streetcars or trams as they were called were the main means of transportation. They passed right outside the dockyard gates making it easy to get around. One problem however was that the top deck of most of them had no roof. Anyone riding up there was exposed to the elements and on a night like this it was misery. Birdie picked up the streetcar right outside the gates and went to go inside. The conductor said, "Sorry we are full up, you'll have to ride on top." Birdie gave a resigned shrug and went to climb the stairs when suddenly he stopped, "Hey," he said to the conductor, "There is a dog in there on a seat." The conductor pointed out that its owner had bought the dog an animal ticket and the rules were it had to ride on a seat. "But," protested Birdie, "I am the only one that needs a seat, surely..." He didn't get any farther, "Either go upstairs or get off." Birdie didn't have much choice. If he got off he would be standing in the rain for fifteen minutes waiting for the next streetcar but if he went upstairs he would be at his destination in not much more than that. He went upstairs. When he arrived at his destination he was soaked to the skin.

He bought the twelve lobsters all alive and kicking and carried them out in the basket provided by the fishmonger. He knew the terminus for the streetcars was only two blocks further on so he walked through the still pouring rain to where the empty streetcar started it's round trip. He got onboard and bought a ticket for himself and then twelve animal tickets. Under the astonished gaze of the conductor he proceeded to put a lobster on each seat with a ticket jammed in its claw. The conductor protested, "You can't do that." Birdie looked down at him, "Try and stop me." The conductor looked him up and down and decided he had better get going.

He rang the bell and the streetcar started out for its first stop, which was outside a cinema. The performance had just finished and the queue in the pouring rain was very long.

When the streetcar stopped there was a concerted rush to get on but Birdie, standing on the platform made sure that only the number needed to fill up the empty seats were allowed in the bottom deck. When he reached this number he physically blocked the entrance for anyone else and pointed upstairs. It didn't take long for someone to spot the lobsters and the riot started. The riot was mainly amongst the queue outside as the limited space at the entrance only permitted two people to be on the platform and it seems there weren't two people prepared to try to physically remove Birdie.

The police car with Birdie and the lobsters arrived on the dock. The two policemen came onboard with Birdie and it was from them we got the story. Birdie was too busy boiling the lobsters. Over an illegal tot of rum the two policemen laughed until the tears came and we had difficulty getting the full story. They said they would dine out on this story for the rest of their lives.

CHAPTER EIGHT

HMS Tartar

We passed the next three months in great discomfort. The ships boilers were not fired up and we only had heat and light from an auxiliary boiler and generator on the dockside. The stokers attended to them but the amount of heat they generated was pitiful. It seemed to rain incessantly and that combined with the food arrangements made life somewhat miserable.

All things must end so in September 38 I was drafted via the depot ship to H.M.S. Cornwall, another County Class cruiser. I thought that it was a case of here we go again but that was not to be. We stayed alongside with a full complement onboard and did nothing but care and maintenance. We did not go to sea and there was the occasional static exercise but it seemed that we were in a state of suspended animation. It appeared that the powers that be were waiting to see what the political future was with Germany before spending any money on preparing for the war that everyone except the politicians thought was coming.

It was a relief when I was promoted to Leading Signalman and drafted to H.M.S. Tartar in March 1939. She was among the first of the Tribal class destroyers who went on to distinguish themselves most nobly in the war. Of the first 16 only one survived the war but their exploits will be long remembered. I had no knowledge of the ship until I arrived in Clydebank where she was just in the final stages of completion.

When I walked onboard and down to the mess I couldn't believe what I saw. It seemed like sheer luxury. Instead of wooden seats and lockers, every seat was padded with a thick vinyl cushion. Instead of a single light bulb glaring over the table there were shielded lights with durable but attractive covers. Instead of the bulkheads being sprayed with cork to absorb the damp, cork that every time a gun fired would scatter all over the mess and into the food, this had a special insulation that stayed in place. Wonder of wonders there was a built in oven heater to keep food warm and heat up food when needed. These may seem small things but to us they were indeed luxury.

For a short time we were billeted ashore until the ship was in all respects ready for sea trials and her turnover from the builder. In April we started the sea trials, which lasted for several weeks. During these trials everything that can possibly be tested is tested from navigation lights to the main armament. The most dramatic of these trials, however, are the speed trials. To ensure that any defect, no matter how small, cannot damage the engines, the trials are carried out in very easy stages. During these runs every aspect of the engines, the shafts and screws and steering mechanism comes under severe scrutiny. The day came for the final speed trials. Up until now the ship had not gone full out although near enough to prove she could meet the challenge.

We left the dock and headed down to the Loch where the trial would commence. We were cruising along when the liner Queen Mary passed us doing her final speed trials and there was much waving and hooting as she passed majestically by. We started to work up and watching the speed log was fascinating. The Queen Mary had left us well behind but as our speed was increased we first kept our distance and then as the Captain ordered increases in revolutions we started to overhaul her. When we passed her we were doing 33 knots and they hooted, waved and cheered. I learned later that the Captain of the Queen Mary was a little chagrined. He had told the distinguished passengers who had the privilege of being onboard during this event, that, his new ship was the fastest ship afloat. It must have been quite a let down to see a destroyer, minuscule in size compared to the Queen Mary, pass him.

We were turned over from the builder and then embarked on what the navy call “Working Up”. This is where every member of the ship’s company including officers learns everything there is to know about the ship in all possible conditions; gunnery, damage control, torpedo firing, submarine hunting and just the physical task of learning to do things by instinct. Time is always of the essence so we had to improve the time taken for every evolution and exercise until the gain of even half a second was considered impossible. It is a demanding and exhausting task but with good leadership the ship’s company knit together into an efficient machine. We were fortunate as the Captain, Officers and Chief and Petty officers were themselves efficient and fair.

It had become obvious that war could not be avoided and the disposition of the ships of the whole Navy both home and abroad was being altered to meet the anticipated threat. In August 1939 we escorted the main battle fleet to Invergordon. It was a fantastic sight and unfortunately the last time the Royal Navy could put together such awesome sea power. The battleships names are now history; Repulse, Royal Sovereign, Royal Oak, Resolution, Rodney together with the full 2nd Cruiser Squadron and flotillas of destroyers assembled for review by the C in C and to provide the opportunity to discuss the future and make appropriate plans.

Our time was as usual occupied with exercises and screening ships detached for exercises until late in August. The fleet was then dispersed to different ports and on the day war was declared we were sitting at anchor in Stornoway.

A strange coincidence occurred to me then. We were sitting round the mess table listening to the BBC and waiting for the announcement we knew was coming at 11 o'clock. I heard a familiar voice and turned to find an old friend of mine from Ganges days coming into the mess. His Captain was visiting ours and he had asked permission to come along to visit. We talked and sat there together and listened to the declaration of war. After a tot of rum and a lively discussion on who was where and what they were doing he left the ship. On V E day I was in the Depot and we were all waiting the announcement that would effectively finish the war in Europe. and the same friend who I hadn't seen throughout the whole of the war, walked in and we listened to the announcement together.

We sailed to rendezvous with part of the fleet on Sept 7th. We were as usual screening the big ships, Nelson, Rodney, Repulse, Ark Royal, Aurora, Sheffield. For a time we screened the Ark Royal who sent up aircraft at dawn and throughout the daylight hours. This duty is a dangerous and hazardous one as the Carrier is totally vulnerable to attack when landing on or flying off aircraft. The destroyers had to use all their speed and manoeuvrability to keep pace with her and move out of her way as she changed courses to take advantage of the wind.

It was during one of these sweeps the enemy sent over their JU88 bombers and one narrowly missed the Ark Royal. This was the first incident that gave rise to the constant claim by the Germans that the Ark Royal had been sunk. The constant theme in their broadcasts after that was to pose the question, "Where is the Ark Royal?" Lord Haw Haw in his English language broadcasts continually told the public that the Ark Royal had been sunk.

Our duty at that time was to intercept any merchant ships whose destination was a port occupied by the Germans. We intercepted quite a few and they were sent into harbour in Scotland to be searched and the goods impounded. Naturally the Germans did not take kindly to this and sent bombers to dissuade us from this activity. Some of the ships were hit by shrapnel and one ship was hit by a bomb that passed through the ship without exploding. The weather was pretty bad so we returned to Scapa Flow. We were in harbour two days when it was decided to try to tempt the enemy into a surface action. The second cruiser squadron, screened by two flotillas of destroyers, sailed into the Skagerrak where it was known several surface units of the German Navy were in harbour. The Tartar was the leading destroyer of the forward screening flotilla and several miles ahead of the main body. We were closed up for action stations and our orders were not to engage but to be pursued back into the guns of our main force.

Radio silence had of course been strictly imposed and the only messages we could receive were sent by Admiralty on the broadcast. The bell from the radio room alerted us to a message and when we read it the orders it contained really shook us. We were advancing into a major battle with units of the German fleet and our main body had turned back a long time ago. We turned and retreated at full speed and fortunately cleared the area before the German units could assemble and give battle.

We wouldn't have lasted more than a few minutes trying to take on a large section of the German navy on our own. It turned out that two destroyers forming the close screen had collided as the visibility was awful and the Admiral had called off the venture. He could not radio us as this would have given away his position and we were out of visual touch. When he was well clear of the area he informed Admiralty who passed the message to us on the broadcast. We returned to Scapa Flow thankful that the Germans had not taken up the challenge. It was the 11th of October 1939 and already we had seen a significant amount of action. We went alongside the oiler and topped up; then went to anchor in the destroyer anchorage.

The Royal Oak was tied up to a buoy close in to the lee of the mainland. During the day there was much going and coming of senior officers as planning for the next phase was carried out. In the early dawn a single German reconnaissance aircraft came over and circled the fleet. I had the morning watch on my own and saw him appear almost out of nowhere. He appeared to be at masthead height and I could see the pilot clearly. I rang the action stations bell but by the time anyone arrived on the bridge he was long gone and I had difficulty convincing anyone of what I had seen. Fortunately an enemy report was generated by one of the Battleships reporting the sighting, so that took me off the hook.

I had the middle watch on the night of the 14th October and, as usual for a destroyer, I was on my own. As we were at anchor the night was expected to be quiet. It was almost 1 o'clock when I heard and felt through my feet a dull explosion. It was impossible to tell from which direction it came but lights and activity appeared onboard the Royal Oak. Our Captain appeared on the bridge with the duty officer and asked me for information. I pointed out the activity on the Royal Oak. Everything seemed under control and the Captain headed down the bridge ladder to turn in again.

About twenty minutes had passed but before he could reach his cabin there was a series of extremely loud explosions and the water borne shock was enormous. The Royal Oak had been hit with torpedoes and to our horror turned on her side and sank within 20 minutes. Twenty-four officers and 809 men died. The immediate assumption was made that a submarine had somehow pierced the defences around Scapa. All destroyers weighed anchor and we spent a fruitless night scouring the anchorage while other destroyers went out through the boom to search the surrounding area with no result.

The Admiralty and German archives tell us that a U Boat commanded by a Lieut. Prien penetrated the defences by sailing on the surface over a sunken block ship and the boom cable. He actually scraped the cable on his way in having very little water below him although he had waited for high tide. He fired a salvo of three torpedoes but only one exploded under the bows of the Royal Oak. It is not known whether it hit the anchor cable but the resulting explosion was only felt slightly onboard and later enquiries elicited the fact that it was believed to be an internal explosion in the paint locker. The submarine withdrew, reloaded his torpedo tubes and fired three more torpedoes. Two of these hit the Royal Oak.

The defective defences of Scapa Flow had been hurriedly patched immediately before the outbreak of war. The section where Priens penetrated and left was awaiting another block ship to be put in position. With tragic irony the block ship arrived the morning after the Royal Oak was sunk. The Admiral withdrew the Fleet and we finished up in Loch Ewe until a detailed survey could be made to ensure the safety of the Scapa Flow anchorage. This security embraced all aspects including anti aircraft protection for the Fleet

Supply bases as well as that of ships. It is impossible for a fleet to operate without an anchorage that provides maximum security yet the money to do this for Scapa Flow had not been forthcoming until after the war started.

We were now detached so that our flotilla consisting of five Tribal destroyers operated in the Northern approaches to deter the enemy from breaking out into the Atlantic and in hunting submarines that were trying to discourage us from this task On one occasion we ran into no less than 4 submerged U Boats and it seemed for a moment that every destroyer was signalling a contact. A lookout on the bridge screamed out "Torpedo Starboard side." I rushed to the side of the Bridge and could see the wakes of two torpedoes approaching. It was impossible for the Captain to take effective avoiding action although he had gone hard to starboard at the first alarm. It is difficult to describe the feeling at a moment like that. Knees tremble, the whole body tightens into itself, breathing stops and the face screws itself up waiting for the noise of the explosion. The torpedoes passed harmlessly underneath. We later learned that the war heads fitted to German torpedoes at this time were both pressure and contact sensitive but the pressure sensitive system was defective also the depth for which they were set was for larger ships so contact was avoided.

We continued at this type of task for weeks on end, always patrolling, screening, hunting submarines and intercepting merchant ships that, even at this late date were trying to make their way into a friendly port. We suffered intensely from the cold in these northern waters. We had not been issued with warm clothing, another economy boob, and as a result we wore any clothing we could lay our hands on. An announcement was made that during this period any rig could be worn including any civilian clothes that were available. The morning after this was announced we were astounded to see one of the seaman take up his look out duties fully equipped for the golf course; plus fours, a tweed jacket, striped socks and hat that looked as if it had been owned by Sherlock Holmes. Nothing was said but it was a moment of light in a gloomy world.

We arrived in harbour in early January 1940; our festive season had been spent chasing submarines. Christmas dinner that year consisted of a mutton chop and two sausages, a peculiar mixture but nevertheless welcome. The signal arrived to go alongside and embark stores and thoughts of real food had the temerity to enter our heads.

It was not to be, we loaded routine stores plus, supposedly, two bales of warm clothing. The crane had swung two massive straw-like bundles on to the upper deck.

They were duffel coats and at first sight we cheered. The Supply Petty Officer attempted to cut through the steel bands that criss-crossed the bundles and had to call on the Boatswain for help. We all stood around watching this exercise and, if the truth be known, making sure we were in line for one of the coats. The Boatswain struggled with an enormous pair of shears and finally released one of the bales. A label attached to one of these was examined and it was learned that these bundles had been made up in 1917 and 1918 and then put in stores. They had turned themselves into one solid mass and no amount of effort could separate one coat from another. The crane was still alongside loading other material and was called on to take back these useless bundles. It took quite a while to convince the Supply Depot that we still had no warm clothing.

During the early part of January we were told to proceed independently and with utmost dispatch to a position just north of Ireland where a merchant ship had sent out a sub sighting report. The weather was superb, flat calm, clear and cold with brilliant sunshine. The position was very near where we were patrolling and in a very short time the ship appeared on the horizon. Through the binoculars I could see a large boat crammed with people floating some distance from the ship.

As we approached a look out on the upper deck warned the U Boat of our approach. The U Boat had tied up alongside the ship and was busily refuelling and taking stores from her. She was on the opposite side to our approach so we knew nothing of this until later. When we were less than three miles from the ship, two aircraft from the Ark Royal who had also been dispatched flew over us and towards the ship. They approached almost at sea level and as they rounded the bows of the ship the U Boat opened fire. He had a sitting target on the first aircraft and it burst into flames and crashed in the sea. The second aircraft veered away, gained height and came back into attack. The U Boat had closed down and was rapidly submerging and the bombs the aircraft dropped fell wide. We arrived on the scene to see the periscope vanish below the surface and we carried out several depth charge attacks but they were inconclusive. The people in the boat were in excellent shape. Apparently the U Boat Commander had been a humane person and had allowed them to get into warm clothing and take with them any personal belongings they could carry. We took them onboard and sank the boat, the ship had been scuttled and was slowly sinking and we watched her go under, a sight I never got used to, despite the number of times I have seen it happen.

We turned, and, obeying our instructions, returned with all dispatch. This trip back was the fastest I have ever travelled in a ship. The log showing the speed ticked steadily upwards until it rested on 42 knots. The Captain of the merchant ship, who had been invited onto the bridge, asked if the log was correct and when told it was his astonishment was very plain although he had spent his life at sea.

There was an unfortunate note to this incident after the war. I was reading the Fleet Air Arm account of this action in a book specially written to cover their exploits. The name of the ship was given but the account was totally inaccurate. According to the historian the people in the boat were barely dressed and in great discomfort in the rough sea. The U Boat captain had bullied them and not allowed them time to gather any warm clothing or life saving material. To make matters worse it claimed that the second aircraft had reported an almost certain sinking of the sub. Since the war I have read so much history that is not only totally wrong but also deliberately distorted.

When we arrived back in harbour at the end of January there was a draft chit for me to report to Devonport barracks for onward routing. It was with very mixed feelings I left the Tartar. We had seen a tremendous amount of action in the first few months of the war. This was a period when the people at home were regarding this as a "phoney" war because ground troops were not involved. The details of all the actions in which we had been involved could not be broadcast. I had many friends and felt that it was the break up of a team.

CHAPTER NINE

HMS Fernie

I travelled in solitary splendour to Devonport and after reporting in was given a few days welcome leave. The short respite came to an end and I was drafted to H.M.S. Fernie. Again I was fortunate in ships. She was a "Hunt" class destroyer, newly commissioned. The name and the class come from the famous foxhunts in England, each ship bearing the name of a particular hunt.

I must explain here why my change of ships was so comparatively frequent. In the signal staff of each ship based on the class of ship there was a clearly laid down complement. This complement was made up in two ways. The first was the rank of the senior man. In a large ship he would be a Chief Yeoman and his signal qualification would be not less than a V S 2, the highest being V S 1. If a Yeoman serving in the same ship was promoted either to a Chief or a V S 1 (the two are not synonymous) he would be drafted immediately to a ship requiring his particular rating or qualification.

This drafting occurred all the way down the line so that every time a promotion occurred it was normal for the man promoted to be drafted from the ship. Promotions in the signal branch were based mostly on the signal qualification held. These started at "Trained operator", V.S.3. V.S.2 and V.S. 1. Each of these qualifications required a course in a signal school lasting up to three months. Once qualified your name was placed on a list for a vacancy to occur in that rating. The lists were very long and it could take several years between promotions. The average age of a Yeoman or Chief Yeoman was in the vicinity of 35.

However, there was a loophole in the regulations. This loophole was, that anyone wishing to take the examination without the course, if passed, would be promoted immediately. This loophole was very rarely used as most men wanted to spend several months ashore waiting for and doing the course. I had volunteered to take what was called the "Fleet" examination each step of the way. The examination papers would be sent from the signal school and opened under supervision on the same day the men doing the course were examined. The examination had to be held on a different ship under officers who had no daily contact with you. The results were sealed and sent back to the school for marking. One of these I remember was held in the Royal Oak.

The transition from peace to war had greatly increased the number of courses and in consequence the number of examination opportunities available. Under war time conditions with no leave, very little to occupy the time between watches I had made a hobby, more or less, of studying the signal books. As a result I was able to make my way very quickly and by the time I was drafted to the Fernie I was an acting Yeoman, which meant I had to undertake the full responsibilities for one year before being confirmed in that position. As this was in April 1940 I was 21 at the time compared to the average age of a Yeoman, as I have said, of 35.

I was the senior member of a staff in which every one was not less than 4 years older and in two cases 18 years older. It was very difficult, particularly since I looked very young even for my age. Initially some of the officers, but thankfully not the Captain, would ask a question of the older hands, ignoring my presence completely. I intervened with an answer, as the information given was incorrect on two occasions and would have altered the ships course incorrectly. The officers soon got the message and such an incident never occurred again.

The duties of a Yeoman in those days do require an explanation. In simple terms he could be described as an interpreter. It was his task to interpret signals no matter how received, flags, semaphore, light, radio Morse or voice and convert them from the code or cypher, into intelligible form for the Captain or whoever was in charge of the ship at the time.

It was necessary for the Yeoman to be on the bridge at all times when the Captain was on the bridge particularly when there were other ships in company. As most Captains spent most of their time on the bridge seated in a special chair behind or alongside the binnacle, it was a very demanding task. The Captain had a sea cabin immediately under the bridge and in a few seconds could be on the bridge. The Yeoman could not be down in the mess as the time taken to get to the bridge, particularly in an emergency, was unacceptable to most Captains. It was necessary therefore to rig up some kind of a bunk, usually immediately under the bridge in the wheelhouse alongside the quartermaster at the wheel. In this way the Captains sea cabin door opened into the wheelhouse and if that did not wake the Yeoman the quartermaster would shake him.

It is difficult to define fully the role of the Yeoman in a ship without appearing to deliberately inflate his importance in the scheme of things. Those who have served will understand the subtle relationship that builds up between a Captain and his Chief Yeoman or Yeoman. It is a relationship, built after getting to know one another, of mutual respect. For example, when with a flotilla, the senior officer will have a signal hoisted in code that means, ships will alter course to Starboard together 45 degrees. The Yeoman will first instruct a signalman to put an answering pendant half way up the mast. He will then interpret the signal to the Captain.

The Captain, after making sure the manoeuvre is possible and practical for his ship to carry out will instruct the Yeoman to acknowledge. The answering pendant is then fully hoisted and when the senior officer hauls down his signal the Yeoman informs the Captain that the signal is executed. The Yeoman had better be right in his interpretation.

It gets much more complicated when manoeuvres are executed that require a great deal of movement. For example, when screening large ships, the positions of the destroyers are clearly defined in screening diagrams each bearing a code number. The signal flying when joining the large ships may say to take up a particular screen. The position of each destroyer in the screening force is reflected in the diagram or may have been allocated before joining the large ships.

No Captain can carry in his head the multitudinous screening and other formations defined in the books for the "Conduct of the Fleet". Furthermore, as ships are moving in close proximity at high speed, the powers that be lay down the recommended way each ship should proceed in order to safely take up their station. Note, I say recommended, as the Captain can carry out the order in what appears to him to be the safest and most practical way under the circumstances prevailing.

Should he, however, take this course of action and it goes wrong, on his head be it. In view of this the adherence to instructions is the usual way. Again, no Captain can possible remember these specific instructions and this is where the Yeoman comes in. First of all, his primary knowledge is the "Conduct of the Fleet." The ability to read flags, semaphore etc, is a very minor part of his job. He must be able to find immediately the appropriate screen, determine where on that screen his ship should be and then inform the Captain exactly what instructions are laid down. In many ships the Yeoman kept in his hooded table a board clearly marked with the points of the compass together with some very small brass ships. In the case of a complicated screen or manoeuvre he could lay out the ships on the board and illustrate the recommended method of taking up position. The Captain would make his decision based on the information and interpretation given to him by the Yeoman.

The first few days or weeks with a new Captain are not easy. He does not wish to doubt your word but at the same time the responsibility is totally his. This gives rise to the polite request "Show me". In this case the Yeoman produces the book with the diagram and reads aloud the instructions. The shorter the period in establishing that the Yeoman knows his job thoroughly the better, as, in rough seas and pouring rain and sometimes in darkness the problem of producing a book and reading it together in a hooded table is very difficult. After a time a subtle relationship develops of mutual respect and trust. This relationship is sometimes resented by some of the officers and sometimes some of the other Chief and Petty Officers because it does give rise to an easy but respectful familiarity not enjoyed by them It is hard to explain that every waking hour and more than that is spent in each others company one becomes totally at ease with the other.

The problem of Captains not being fully familiar with correct manoeuvring has been with the Navy for many years and has resulted in some horrific collisions, particularly when taking up screening positions. This is of course due to the fact that there are simply not enough ships in the Royal Navy to enable commanding officers to spend enough time at sea and become totally familiar with the complications of manoeuvring and ship handling let alone keep up to date with signal books. In one case where the Court Martial found a Captain guilty of hazarding his ship the Court stated the Captain had been given bad advice. In other words the signal had been interpreted incorrectly and he had turned the ship to Starboard instead of Port at a particularly critical moment of changing the screen.

Wartime made this situation doubly hazardous as in the necessary rapid expansion of the Navy Officers who had left the Navy at a relatively early age on achieving the rank of Lieutenant or Lieut. Commander. Wealthy families would have a son trained by the Navy but when he reached a certain age, say 30; they would get him to resign. He would then return to the family activities, which could be business, farming as gentlemen farmers or simply enjoying travel and the social life. It certainly did not include keeping up to date with signal books or ship handling.

Being recalled into the Navy they were given very little reorientation instructions and found themselves as Captains or First Lieutenants of small ships such as destroyers. They would sail in company with other destroyers with experienced Captains and be expected to carry out every type of manoeuvre correctly.

Despite the fact that the Fernie was a brand new ship, her Captain, whilst only a Lieutenant had several years of experience in destroyers and when I discovered this I breathed a sigh of relief. It was not necessary to dot every "I" and cross every "T" when signals arrived. The result was that I was rapidly assimilated into the scene and within a short time I could make an interpretation that was immediately accepted without question.

The design of this class of ship was to me, most peculiar. Despite the fact that the designers had known the armament and the engine room requirements would need a ships company of a given size, the living accommodation was cramped beyond belief. The ships galley (cookhouse) was far too small and the arrangements for cooking and providing meals were pitiful.

The Bridge was a huge flat expanse with the binnacle and navigators table and the signalman's table on the forward bulkhead. When the ship rolled, and boy did she roll, there was nothing to grab on to unless you were near the bridge rail. I watched numerous members of the ship's company, both officers and men, lose their balance and come up with a bone-shaking bang at the other side. It was the only ship I ever served in, that, when new seamen came onboard and served as lookouts on the bridge, I had to go round and assure them it wasn't going to turn over. At first they took some convincing and their look of absolute terror as they hung on to the rail as she went through her paces was awful to see.

The enemy had entered into an intense period of mine laying both by aircraft and by ship. They were laying several types of mines; moored mines, magnetic mines, acoustic mines and were achieving a degree of success. Mine countermeasures such as degaussing of ships to avoid triggering magnetic mines took time. Minesweeping to permit convoys to sail in and out of the major ports such as London, delayed our sailing on many occasions. Our losses due to these mines were not insignificant. Watching a ship go up in flames, as we had to many times, was horrible and frustrating. On one occasion as we were clearing the Thames a wooden minesweeper ahead of us seemed to dissolve into a cloud of smoke and when it cleared there was literally nothing to see except splintered wood. There were no survivors. The feeling you get on these occasions, as you pass over the same water where obviously mines have been laid, is indescribable.

The war on land was not going very well during those first months of 1940 but we hardly noticed. We were totally preoccupied with trying to get convoys safely through the channel and half way across the Atlantic. The Atlantic convoys were weeks of intense drudgery punctuated by moments of intense action. The U Boats, when they attacked, would mostly attack at night and despite our constant patrol and search, the first intimation of their presence would be a shocking underwater vibration as their torpedoes found a target. We would scurry around trying to locate them with our ASDIC equipment but it is a big ocean and they would rapidly take evading action. Many times we would circle the wounded ship and watch them abandon ship as best they could. Other ships, designated as rescue ships, would close in on the survivors if possible and pick them up.

There was one incident which, even today, if I close my eyes I can see it as it was then. We had closed on a ship hit by a torpedo. The name on her stern was "Vancouver". She was obviously carrying highly inflammable cargo as the flames were reaching and roaring upwards We circled her, all the time sounding for U Boats. Through the binoculars I could see the crew trying to abandon ship in the middle of that inferno. The wind was blowing from bow to stern and keeping the forecastle a little clear of the fire but the fire was moving inexorably forward. I could see a man standing as far forward as he could and he was waving frantically at us to come closer. He could see us clearly in the light of the fire. We obviously could not approach without both endangering the ship and the convoy. I watched until a sudden rush of flame engulfed him and he vanished.

It was on one of these Atlantic convoys I had another lesson in the frailty of human conduct. We had an extremely large convoy, and, because of a warning about surface raiders such as the Bismarck we had a battleship with a Flag officer in charge of the escort. We, of course, were very small fish and were stationed well out on the starboard quarter of the merchant ships keeping constant vigil for submarines. The senior officer of the destroyers flashed a message originated by the Flagship to all ships in company.

He asked if anyone could decode a specific message we had all received on the broadcast by its routing it was intended for the Flag officer. Under these circumstances only the ship to which it was addressed would decode or decipher the message. We were far too busy to attempt to read other people's mail. The Captain told the wireless office to send a copy to the bridge, which of course they did. After examining the message, which was quite long, he asked me if I had any ideas.

At first I was really puzzled as the only code it resembled was a merchant ship code. Then I had an idea. A long time ago in a session with other senior communicators one of them had posed a question, which was, "If all naval codes and cyphers are considered compromised how would you communicate with ships at sea without using any of them". None of us knew but the questioner produced an obscure instruction to cover this situation. It said that the message should be encrypted as usual but the result instead of being transmitted should be re-encrypted using a merchant navy signal system that everyone carried but was very rarely used.

I took the message and went down below to work on it. Sure enough, this is exactly what had happened. I decrypted the message and it turned out to be a diversion of course for the convoy to avoid a wolf pack that had been sighted on our present course. When I took it back on the bridge the Captain was really pleased and he had great pleasure in signalling via the senior destroyer that we had a plain language version of the message. Instead of passing it through him by light we were told to close on the flagship and pass it by light directly ourselves. This we did.

On completion, a course amendment was signalled and the convoy turned to avoid the U Boats. After this was done we received a signal from the Flagship congratulating the ship and asking for the name, rank, etc of the person responsible. I then received a personal signal from the Flagship congratulating me and informing me that a report on this would be sent to Admiralty. The normal books had been compromised by what had been thought to be the loss of a ship. This turned out to be a false alarm but it did wake everybody up. As months went by and I heard no more of the incident I assumed Admiralty was too busy to write me at least a letter of commendation.

A long time later I met the Chief Yeoman who was serving in the Flagship at the time. He remembered the incident well and I told him I had expected to hear about it but never did. He said, "And you never will, we had a Flag Lieutenant with the Admiral and it was his job to forward the report with your name. Can you imagine a Flag Lieutenant who is supposed to know all about signals sending a report to Admiralty telling them the convoy would have been in hazard due to his lack of knowledge and he had to ask for help." This was another example of the human frailty that existed due to the overwhelming desire for promotion by concealing shortcomings, usually at someone else's expense.

In early 1940 there was very little, if any danger of air attack in the Atlantic due to the distances involved and our whole efforts were devoted to the protection of the convoys and the destruction of U Boats. While ships in convoy during this period could be and were protected extremely well to the extent that losses were few, the sinking of ships that were routed independently was devastating. In February alone in 1940 we lost 45 ships totalling nearly 170,000 tons. To hear over the distress frequency the cries for help and not be able to respond was terribly frustrating. In my minds eye I could see with each call, the "Vancouver" over and over again.

Towards the beginning of May we were ordered to take up Channel convoy duty. The land war was going against us and the army was fighting a rearguard action trying to establish a new line of defence where they could dig in and fight back. The Germans were trying to cut off their supply line and the Channel convoys were coming under frequent attack. The enemy attacks had been quite successful despite the fact that our fighter bases were near enough to give us protection. I was puzzled at the lack of air cover because the dive-bombers and other bombers would be on us, we were almost like sitting ducks.

In the middle of a fierce attack when all our guns would be blazing and we were dodging and weaving as much as the narrow channel would allow, the fighters would arrive and the battle turn into an air battle. Due to this we often found ourselves opening fire on friendly aircraft as they arrived in the middle of the battle.

It took some time but this situation gradually changed and the convoy when passing through particular areas would have fighter cover but we had many losses before that. During May it seemed that the number of air attacks appeared to be reduced. Later I learned that the enemy had diverted a large number of his aircraft to attacks on Norway. The mine laying however continued and the minesweepers plied their deadly trade to clear every harbour ready for our arrival or to enable us to sail. Sometimes they would take station ahead of the outgoing convoy and sweep. We would follow in their tracks and hope they did not miss any. After a night of mine laying by the enemy, particularly around the Thames, the exploding mines as they were swept did nothing to console us. However we were fortunate because despite the large number of ships passing over mined waters our losses were very few.

These comparatively few losses were due to two factors. One was the magnetic mine countermeasure that had been rapidly introduced by changing the magnetic signature of the ships and the other was the shortage of magnetic mines in the hands of the enemy. In the first four months of the war, however, our losses due to magnetic mines had been very heavy, particularly down the East Coast of England. The minesweepers towed a floating cable through which an electrical current was passed to imitate the magnetic field of a ship. The mine would explode, usually just astern of these floating cables. Sometimes however it would explode at the beginning or the middle of the cables and the minesweeper would suffer damage and the cables would be destroyed.

Towards the end of May it became obvious that the Army were now fighting a rearguard action to reach the ports in and around Dunkirk. On the 20th "Operation Dynamo" commenced which was the name given to the evacuation of Dunkirk and nearby ports. Every available ship, including destroyers, was being sent and we found ourselves guarding convoys with only ourselves as escort and over our heads an almighty battle was taking place. The story of Dunkirk and the evacuation from those ports is too well known to repeat and the operation officially ended on the 4th June, an incredible feat. According to the official archives it had been hoped that 45 thousand men might be rescued. On completion, over 366 thousand were brought home.

As Dunkirk captured the imagination and the headlines it deserved, there were still thousands of troops who were fighting inland between Dunkirk, Le Havre and Cherbourg. In the early part of June, after the main evacuation the Fernie was ordered to patrol the coast towards Cherbourg. They had anticipated that some of our troops would be arriving in the vicinity of the ports and beaches in that area.

We patrolled close in to try and observe and determine the situation, and encountered shelling from shore batteries on the cliffs near St. Valery. We replied with considerable vigour and could see our shells exploding around the area from which the gunfire seemed to come. I was surprised to see the fall of shot being less than three quarters of the distance between us and the shore. I don't know what they were using for artillery but it obviously could not reach the distance our guns could and did.

We carried on down the coast, visibility was poor and we were constantly at action stations in case we encountered a sea borne enemy. I later learned that a massive attempt to bring troops off from St. Valery had almost failed due to the extremely bad visibility encountered. It was also recorded that in this area occurred the only instance where a large body of troops had fought their way back to the sea and the Navy was unable to rescue them.

In the middle of June we were ordered into Cherbourg to pick up stragglers, the main evacuation from Cherbourg and the other adjacent ports had been completed when we arrived. As we entered the port the bombers were busily bombing the fort that stood at the entrance with the idea, I suppose, of trapping anyone they could inside. I must admit I wasn't too enthusiastic about going in.

We pulled alongside a concrete quay; certainly, no words of mine can ever convey fully the scene that faced us. As far as the eye could see was a graveyard of vehicles of every kind. Bren gun carriers, troop transports, supply vehicles, ambulances, motorbikes canteen trucks, army coloured automobiles even bicycles. Our orders were to pick up any stragglers then demolish as much as we could of the ports facilities.

A group of soldiers cheered us as we pulled alongside; they thought they had missed their chance to be evacuated. There was a Brigadier General and two or three other officers and about twenty men. We had berthed in a cargo unloading area and there were huge cranes towering over us as well as on the whole length of the quay. Our demolition team went ashore with the intention of rendering these huge cranes useless by blowing away one of the tripod legs supporting them. They started at the far end of the quay planting fused explosives, the further away the shorter the fuse.

Several members of the ship's company were given permission to land and see what they could find in the way of machine guns and ammunition. One thing we lacked on the bridge was firepower and it was considered that a couple of Bren guns mounted there would be a great idea. They did not restrict themselves to machine guns and soon we had several motorbikes piled against the funnel together with an enormous amount of other contraband they found in the abandoned vehicles. An amusing aside in all this was the NAAFI vans loaded with cigarettes and chocolates and all the other goodies. Naturally they made a beeline for these and our canteen manager was furious. He knew it would be a long time before he sold any more cigarettes or chocolate.

The enemy had not been idle and was bombing the area surrounding the port but not the port itself at that moment. This soon changed and a whole formation of high-level bombers arrived overhead. They started on that most devastating method of bombing; pattern bombing. They lined up more or less abreast covering an awful lot of sky and at timed or signalled intervals released bombs as they moved over the port. I watched them approach through my binoculars and as they flew, the area they left behind was totally destroyed.

It became obvious that within a few minutes we would be in the centre of the next salvo. The order was given to take cover but there is no cover on an open bridge. I, like everyone else on the bridge fell flat on our faces with our steel helmets covering the backs of our heads. I feel sure my nose made a hole in the deck as I tried to make myself as small as possible. There was that unforgettable howling scream made by falling bombs followed by ear splitting and ground shaking explosions. The quay on our port side about 200 yards away vanished in a dust cloud. Debris came hurling down on us but no one was hurt and miracle of miracles it became obvious they had run out of bombs as they disappeared in the distance.

The demolition party rushed back onboard and reported all fuses set so the Captain gave the order for them to be lit. This meant that the Leading Seaman in charge had to retrace his steps and light the fuses with the furthest away being the first, of course. We had no remote control devices. He accomplished this and jumped onboard over the guard rail as the first crane exploded and toppled into the water. The Captain ordered the last hawser to be cast off and we went slowly astern to clear the quay. Suddenly a shout went up and, making their way through the trucks we saw four soldiers screaming and waving. We had cleared the quay by a few feet and the Captain turned to the senior army officer and demanded an explanation. The man shook his head and said, "You will have to leave them."

The Captain had been, of course, taking a very careful note of the time. He wanted to be well clear before the two cranes towering over us blew up. It was an unforgettable moment, he looked at me, cocked his eyebrow, shrugged his shoulders then ordered "stop both engines" then "half ahead". Everything seemed to go in to slow motion. The expressions of the army officers registered absolute bewilderment; the ship appeared to move sluggishly forward as its bows came level with the quay. The soldiers racing down the quay didn't seem to be gaining any ground. He ordered "starboard ten" and then "midships" then "stop engines" and we scraped along the jetty sending up sparks like a dozen welders torches. The first soldier practically fell over the guard-rail rapidly followed by the other three and, of all things, a dog.

The order was given for full astern and as we started to make stern way, the crane at our bows blew up. It fell in the water not ten yards ahead and a huge chunk of concrete fell on our forecastle but no one was hurt. We were clear of the quay when the second one blew and then we had sufficient room to turn and head out of harbour. The enemy was still bombing the fort then diverted their attention to us but the bombs fell clear and the barrage we put up discouraged them. We were the last ship to leave Cherbourg.

Once clear of the port but still at action stations the damage assessment was carried out. The concrete block on the forecastle was far too large to move so we had to wait until it would be removed by crane when alongside wherever we were going. All other damage was superficial and no one was injured. The four soldiers were sent for and appeared on the bridge for the Captain to speak to them. They stood rigidly to attention and before the Captain could speak one of them said, "Thank you sir for coming back." He nodded and then asked them why they had not come onboard when we first arrived with the other soldiers. He suspected that they had been searching for anything of value they could find. He was astounded when the first soldier nodded towards the Army officer and said, "But we were ordered to by the Major, he told us to sabotage as many vehicles as we could and get onboard before the ship sailed. We thought we would have been warned by a siren or something."

The army officer said nothing and the Captain sent the men below. He did not address the Major but carried on conning the ship as if nothing had occurred. After a time the Major approached him to speak but the Captain turned to him and very politely requested him to leave the bridge, which he did. Nothing more was said about the incident. The dog meanwhile had been making friends with everyone he met. He was brought up to the bridge and went into a paroxysm of tail wagging and jumping. He was thin and scrawny; they called him Cherbourg. In a very short time he was fat, sleek and totally spoiled and believed that every sailor was a source of food. We could not land him in England because of the rabies regulations. He was still there, fat dumb and happy when I left the ship.

CHAPTER TEN

Routine!

We returned to Portsmouth and landed the soldiers and, unfortunately we had to give up the Bren guns and all the other goodies that had been retrieved. The ships company took a very dim view of it but with the desperate shortages created by the evacuation it made a lot of sense.

We returned to our convoy escort duty but with the enemy able to launch attacks from so close now that France had fallen it became hazardous in the extreme. During the following three months attacks were constant and prolonged in the Channel. The RAF did their best but our losses mounted and every trip became somewhat of a nightmare. To add to this there was no real respite when alongside as the ports were under attack at night and we found ourselves joining the local AA defence batteries with our guns. The attacks by incendiaries spread over wide areas, meant that we had to land support people in the dockyard to assist in putting out the large number of fires that were started. It may sound crazy but I was always relieved when we went to sea. At least we had sea room and didn't feel like a sitting duck.

The enemy then brought E boats into the action. These fast moving torpedo boats attacked at night and we had little if anything to defend us from this new threat. We lost far too many ships, as our convoys were quite large with very limited escort. The number of ships in convoy was reduced to a manageable 10 but the runs had to be more frequent so there was no respite and an immediate turn around became the routine.

The battle for the control of the Channel was going forward rapidly on both sides and we realised this on a convoy at the beginning of August. It was a glorious day with light cloud scudding overhead and a sky as blue as nature could make it. There was no sign of the enemy aircraft and every minute that passed without an attack was a minute gained. Suddenly, without the usual warning sounds of enemy aircraft, the screaming howl we always associated with bombs hit our ears and the water in and around the convoy exploded in huge water spouts. We desperately searched the skies to find a target but we could not see one. Again came the scream and again the water erupted all around the convoy.

So far no one had been hit but the shrapnel was flying across the deck and burying itself in the safety mats around the bridge. One piece as big as my fist penetrated the mats and the steel bulkhead in front of me and jammed there smoking. If it had managed to come right through we would have had many casualties on the bridge. Every minute or so we had to endure this massive bombardment with the utter frustration of not knowing where the enemy was in order to defend ourselves.

A message then came through from the Vice Admiral Dover telling us we were being shelled by the guns at Cap Gris Nez. The Germans had mounted long-range guns and we, having to stick to a swept channel were sitting ducks. We were twenty miles from the French coast so accuracy when firing at a specific target was not good but they could and did plant their shells in and around the convoy.

It may sound incredible but we even became accustomed to this. However the convoy timing was changed to put us through this area at night. It may have given someone in Admiralty a psychological boost but for us it was a waste of time. The enemy reconnaissance knew where we were, they knew the speed of the convoy and could predict with absolute certainty when we would be within killing range. The only difference the night made was that we could now see the flash of the guns as they fired and count the seconds until the shells hit. Not exactly an improvement to our situation. It turned out that we came into range at a certain point in the Channel and from the flash to the explosion would take 64 seconds. As we moved along the time element stretched out and when it reached 72 seconds it stopped. However the time taken by the convoy to cover the distance from entering the shelling zone to leaving it seemed like hours. Occasionally when it seemed as if one of our ships was in trouble we had to go back into the zone to check up. Despite this action, by the enemy, the shelling had little effect and casualties were very small for the effort expended.

Towards the end of September we had a break in the convoy routine. We were ordered to rendezvous with other destroyers in the Channel after taking onboard an Admiral. We arrived at the rendezvous. It turned out there were six of us under the command of the Admiral. Why he picked our ship to make his command ship I never found out, as we were not the senior officers by any means. It was dusk and we headed in the general direction of the French coast, a rather unhealthy place to be in view of the German occupation. By the time we had formed up it was quite dark.

We were in single line doing about twenty knots. There was much discussion on the bridge involving the Admiral, the Captain and the Gunnery officer. They had their heads buried under the hooded tables and were talking about the ranges and bearings of positions on the charts they were studying. There had been meetings ashore on the previous two days but no signals had been made that could give any indication of the operation upon which we were embarked. However it became obvious to me that we were heading for some area or port to bombard it; that was the only possible conclusion.

Normally the Captain, once we had sailed, would inform the ship's company what we were heading into. This time nothing had been said and needless to say I was bombarded with questions, as the assumption was that in my position I knew everything that was going on. This was usually true but I never under any circumstances revealed it until after the Captain had made his announcement; I could then and did discuss it freely. I always considered it absolute arrogance on the part of officers who told the ships company nothing but expected them to go blindly where they were led. I am afraid in some ships it was the rule rather than the exception.

The Admiral was pacing up and down at the back of the bridge as we steamed along. One of the lookouts, new to the navy and new to the ship, a man about 35 years old, leaned over and violated every rule in the book. He tapped the Admiral on the shoulder and the startled Admiral turned on him as if he had been shot. In a very polite voice he asked "Where are we going and what are we doing sir?" The Admiral burst out in fury, "Mind your own business. What is your name?" The lookout gave his name and then added, "It is as much my bloody business as it is yours, it's my life you know."

I heard every word of the exchange and the Admiral went to the front of the bridge and furiously recounted the incident to the Captain. He insisted that when convenient the man should be charged with insubordination. The Captain demurred slightly by explaining to the Admiral that he had always briefed the ship's company once we were at sea regarding our operational orders. This did not mollify the Admiral who shrugged off the Captain's possible excuse for the man.

Just then the First Lieutenant joined us on the bridge and the Captain briefed him in front of the Admiral with the intention of getting the disciplinary action off on the right track. The First Lieutenant said "Oh this is going to be interesting," the Admiral asked why and the First Lieutenant replied that the man in question had only been in the ship two days and in civil life he was an extremely wealthy and well known lawyer. The navy had tried, when he volunteered to make him accept a commission but he had refused. He wanted to serve on the lower deck. "I expect he will push this thing up to a court martial, yes it is going to be interesting", he said. For some strange reason we heard nothing more about the case after we returned to harbour.

We arrived at the entrance to the French (to this day I cannot remember it's name) harbour around midnight and entered in line ahead. As we were the lead ship we opened fire first, and, as we were using flashless cordite it was impossible for the enemy to know from where the shells were being fired. The whole line of destroyers circled the harbour pouring literally hundreds of rounds into the port and its facilities. The explosions and resulting fires were enormous. Oil tanks went up in a blaze, buildings caught fire and burned turning the night sky a brilliant red. We had done a half circle and were now clearing the harbour and not a single shot had been fired in return. Every other ship had the same story. The enemy had mistaken our attack for an air bombing attack and had put up a useless barrage of anti aircraft fire.

We returned to harbour with destroyers breaking off to go to their own ports throughout the night. The Admiral left the ship in the early light of dawn. We never heard a word of congratulations on an operation that was totally successful.

We returned to our usual routine and we really knew very little of the larger picture of the war involving the big ships and the home fleet. We were then called upon to escort two of the large minelayers to lay a protective mine barrier around the south coast. They were capable of speeds far higher than we were able to do and could even lay mines at high speed. They were, apparently, laying a new type of mine that had tentacles spread out in all directions. A touch on one of these exploded the mine.

The operation was a total failure. As fast as they laid the mines they exploded and this went on for ages. Finally they decided enough was enough and we were ordered to return. I must say we steered well clear of them on the way back. It was obvious that whatever mines they had tried to lay were extremely touchy. This effort to lay new types of mines and find means of sweeping them was a constant battle. When we thought we had the measure of every mine they could lay by ship and aircraft a new one would emerge. The new one during this period was the acoustic mine which exploded at the sound of a passing ship.

This caused a great deal of havoc until one was recovered and the frequency at which it operated was analysed. Minesweepers were then fitted with equipment that transmitted sound waves, we were also fitted with a similar device that, when it was working, sounded more like a drum than a ships engine. However it seemed to work. The reduced size convoys plodded on and the air force did a marvellous job of defending us. The enemy bombers and their fighter escort would arrive but they had been detected and our fighters would be over us before they reached us. We watched the air battles, unable to fire for fear of hitting our own aircraft. The sound of machine guns, like ripping hard cloth was constant and an aircraft would break away with smoke pouring from it and head in a screaming dive into the ocean. We tried to identify the type of aircraft but it's speed of descent and the smoke made it very difficult. Naturally we always hoped it was the enemy.

Sometimes the pilot of a fighter aircraft would bail out and sometimes members of bomber crews would be seen swinging from parachutes. When this happened I was ordered to get on the VHF set and tell RAF operations room our exact position supplied by the navigator. On one occasion I watched a pilot descending in his parachute not knowing whether he was RAF or German. I was soon enlightened as, out of the cloud came a clearly identifiable Messerschmidt who proceeded to do a machine gun run at the helpless pilot. I could not tell if he was hit but the action was so cold-blooded it made every nerve in my body shake. This is the only time I witnessed such a vicious violation of the rules of humanity although others to whom I recounted the story said they had seen it happen.

The routine of convoy duty in the Channel continued on and we became familiar with specific ships that were engaged in the coastal run. When the convoy list was supplied I would go over it to see if there were any old familiars. Usually there was and we would be pleased at some and groaned at others. Some kept their speed and distance and in the morning you would find them safely tucked into their appropriate column. Others would wait for darkness and then crack on speed to get way ahead of the convoy giving us all sorts of anxious times. Some could never keep up and by daybreak would be miles astern with all the attendant problems. The convoys were designated by speed so that we would have a 7 knot convoy or a 10 knot convoy etc,. These speeds were based on the fastest speed that could be maintained by the slowest ship in the convoy. Needless to say for those that could travel faster the temptation to do so was great. For those who had claimed they could maintain the speed but could not straggled behind and were sitting ducks for the bombers unless we could get to them and round them up.

Winter with its cold sleet and high winds was upon us. The Channel can be a rough taskmaster in bad weather and, except in fog, the bombers seemed unaffected, adding to our misery as we plodded along. Just before Christmas we set off with another convoy. We had hoped that we would get some break at this time. We were angry, the ship's company felt they deserved a break and Christmas would give the powers that be an excuse to leave us alone for a couple of days. I realise now that the war at sea was taking a tremendous toll on Britain and every conceivable means to keep supplies flowing had to be used. Even so I found it difficult to accept.

We had taken onboard special supplies of food to celebrate Christmas and there was talk of Turkey and Xmas pudding etc, which helped to lift the gloom. It was the night before Christmas and we were plodding along, lifting slightly to the motion of the sea and the sky was like black velvet punctuated with a fantastic number of brilliant stars. It was cold and I was shrugged down into my clothes and tucked in the corner of the bridge to avoid the keen wind. The forward gun was manned as usual but not fully as we were not at action stations.

Sound carries a long way over water so at night everything is hushed. This enables us to hear the sound of engines in the air or on the sea. It was midnight and suddenly from the forward gun a voice was raised in song, "Oh Holy Night". The Officer of the Watch rushed to the front of the bridge ready to order silence but the Captain held up his hand to stay him and we listened. In that setting we were in a cathedral with a boy soprano whose voice climbed to the rafters celebrating the arrival of Christianity's holiest day. The singer turned out to be just that. He had been a boy soprano in a famous cathedral {he still wasn't far from being a boy) and he could not resist the urge to welcome Christmas in the only way he knew how.

Christmas dinner at sea with all the watch keeping to be done and total sobriety the order of the day, is not up to much. I never did meet a naval cook who knew how to cook a Turkey properly. It was incredible however how a few hardy souls, refusing to be denied their celebration can conjure up a Christmas tree from a broom handle and a variety of whiskers, decorate the mess with hanging streamers made from toilet rolls etc. There were of course those who had saved their tots to get an extra bang out of the day, but even they were careful not to overdo it knowing that at any minute they might be fighting for their lives against a totally sober enemy.

It was early in January of 1941, the 8th I think it was, when, in the Channel, just beyond the Thames estuary the lookout reported aircraft. I turned and the aircraft was over the land but coming towards us in a slow side slipping motion. The aircraft was painted sky blue underneath, which indicated it belonged to ferry command who delivered repaired aircraft to the different air bases.

I watched the aircraft circling and getting ever lower and it was clear the Pilot was in deep trouble as the engines kept cutting out and reviving. Suddenly the Pilot made up his mind and put the aircraft down on the sea between us and another small escort vessel, the "Haslemere". It hit the sea like a pancake and skidded along a little way then began to sink. The door on the starboard side opened and I caught a clear view of the pilot dressed in what appeared to be black leather. The Pilot jumped and the aircraft sank creating turbulence so I could not see what had happened to the pilot.

The Haslemere was quite close and a man dived over the side with a rope tied around his waist. It was impossible to make out the details of what was happening until we saw members of the crew of the Haslemere pulling their crew member back onboard. It was the Captain who had dived and unfortunately he was dead when they brought him back in. It may have been the frigid water or some other cause but he died in his attempt to save the pilot.

There was very little wreckage, and what there was, had been scooped up by the escort vessel. They had launched a whaler and it came alongside with the material it had rescued. As the senior officer of the escort I suppose they felt it was the duty of our Captain to examine the material and make the necessary report. The most puzzling item was a ladies handbag that was opened first. The contents were completely dry and he laid them out on the hooded table. There was all the usual things a woman would carry in her bag, keys, lipsticks etc. He opened the wallet and I heard him gasp quite audibly. He turned to the curious onlookers, myself included, and said: "It was Amy Johnson."

You may not have heard of Amy Johnson but in Britain her name and fame were as well known as Amelia Earhart. Her exploits had brought her not only fame but also a great affection from the people of Britain. Songs were written about her, in fact at school we had had an Amy Johnson day when she had once again achieved a notable flying feat. It was like hearing of the death of an old friend and we were all devastated

The Captain called me over and dictated a message to Admiralty so I had the tragically and unforgettable duty of notifying Britain of the loss of one of it's most famous and loved daughters. She was working for Ferry command like many other women pilots and was on her way to deliver the aircraft to an air station. No one ever determined what went wrong with the aircraft and her body was never recovered. I had been writing poetry for a long time. This was a hobby I pursued whenever we had a quiet moment. That afternoon as we resumed our station on the convoy, I scribbled on a signal pad the following: -

AMY JOHNSON

When the last all clear is sounded over
these ravaged lands, and the victory parades
follow the sound of marching bands,
You will not be there.
You will be lying here asleep, in England's
all protecting keep, and the ever moving
waves will wash gently o'er your grave.
In such honourable company.
In the years that follow, on each Remembrance Day,
the mourning multitudes will stand silently to pray,
The plaintive notes of the last post will
echo through the land, and the waves will
sound your threnody over the golden sand.
Then you will be there.

For some reason, after the war, several authors writing about the war mentioned the "Mysterious death" of Amy Johnson. I have read that she bailed out with two others that she was carrying on a secret mission. I have read that she was shot down in France after a clandestine trip to assist the French underground. These stories and others have been printed, and, I expect, have been believed by people. I have no idea why this distortion of facts occurs. I have read several, so called, authoritative accounts by historians on incidents that occurred while I was there that bear absolutely no relation to the actual facts

Tribal Destroyer 'Tartar' in which I was serving when the war started.

'Hunt' class destroyer 'Fernie' in which I was serving during the evacuation from France in 1940.

H.M.S. Wallace in which I spent over three years during the war after leaving 'Fernie'. It is the destroyer in which I served with Phillip.

Naturally, in my 35 years I served in many ships, most are mentioned but the 'Tartar', 'Fernie', and 'Wallace' are the one's in which I spent the war at sea.

Photogarph of the model H.M.S. Wallace taken in 1942 as our souvenir

The refurbished model of H.M.S Tartar after I found it with the Captain's daughter - Lady Hartington.

'On the Bridge'.

Lieut. Commander Edward Gavin Heywood Lonsdale D.S.C. And bar R.N.

To whom the model of H.M.S. Wallace was presented. A superb officer and gentleman.

Lieutenant Phillip Mountbatten (now the Duke of Edinburgh)

Author (1945) after leaving H.M.S. Wallace

Ganges football team (1934)

(Author front row right)

H.M.S Ganges Mast

CHAPTER ELEVEN

HMS Wallace

We arrived back in our home port, and to my astonishment and considerable dismay there was a draft chit waiting for me. I could not understand why. I had been in the ship less than a year. As far as I knew I had no problems yet a new Yeoman walked onboard to take over when we arrived alongside. He was an old timer and when I asked him he had no idea either. He had been in the barracks and suddenly, with no warning, he was on his way to meet the ship. He was married with a wife in the port and he was not at all happy to the extent that he almost blamed me.

I sorted out the messages that the despatch rider had brought and took them down to the Captain. He leafed through them until he came to the signal notifying about the transfer. He looked at me and asked me why I wanted to leave the ship. I breathed a sigh of relief realising that the move had nothing to do with him. I told him I not only knew nothing about it but also was very upset at having to leave to which he replied, "So am I." I told the Captain that the new Yeoman was on the upper deck and he told me to ask him to come down which I did.

He could get no more from him than I could and expressed the opinion it was a drafting error and to do nothing until he had chance to get on the telephone. We went down to the mess and naturally the new Yeoman was quite upset at his reception. An hour later I was sent for and the Captain told me that there was nothing he could do about the move. Apparently the orders had come down, not from the drafting office, but from the Directorate of Communications in Admiralty and no one could change their minds. We shook hands and he assured me of his complete satisfaction with my performance and he would reflect that in his report.

I went to the mess and packed and was on the jetty less than an hour later after all the farewells. I felt devastated. I had no idea where I was going except to the barracks. I was at a complete loss at this arbitrary treatment and I felt terribly alone. The truck arrived and complete with baggage I was taken to the barracks. On arrival I reported to the Signal section where the Chief greeted me with the comment, "It's about time". That was the last straw and I unleashed a burst of invective that should have taken his ears off. People in the regulating office stood around in astonishment at hearing a very young Yeoman blasting a very senior Chief.

He put his hand up to calm me down and then ushered me into his private office where he told me to sit down and have a cigarette. I did this with ill grace and started to speak again. He waved his hand for quiet and I shut up. "I am sorry" he said, "I have been having phone calls about you for the last three days, I did not know where you were until this morning." It turned out that he was a Chief who had retired before the war and had been given this job as he was really too old to go to sea. He had total sympathy for people like myself, and he fully understood that the life we were living removed almost completely the normal disciplinary fear of our seniors. We were living on the edge and had no time for useless formalities, criticism or sarcasm and reacted as I had to his unthinking comment.

He handed me a folder with my travel orders. It contained food vouchers for possible overnight stays in a hotel or boarding house; a rail ticket to Rosyth in Scotland with orders to report onboard a ship called H.M.S. Wallace at Rosyth. I had to go over to the pay office and sign for an advance of pay plus travel claim expense sheets. I had to pay out of my own money and then claim it back; a process that took months. When I arrived at the pay office I asked for a travel advance against a future claim. This shook them up a bit as they did not like to play it that way. The Pay Sub Lieutenant refused and offered me an advance against my own pay. I, very politely asked him his name, he asked why. I told him I was going over to the mess and would stay there until I had the money to travel. I then pushed the travel order at him and asked him to ring the regulating office and explain why I would be staying.

He was furious and frankly I wondered if I had pushed too far and in fact I wondered why I had pushed at all. It dawned on me that I was looking at these routine things and the people charged with operating them with absolute disdain. My mind had become accustomed to the fundamentals of trying to stay alive and I couldn't care less about the people who stayed ashore in order to keep us at sea despite the fact they were essential to all of us.

Before I could turn away he told me to wait and within a few minutes he was back with five pounds and a receipt slip, which I signed. The transport took me, and my unpacked baggage, to the railway station where I embarked on a train for Edinburgh. On the journey the train was packed even in the corridors. It seemed as if we were stopped at every station for ages. The bombing was causing severe disruption to the rail service and the movement of goods took precedence over passengers so we were shunted into sidings to let the goods trains pass. A journey that normally took between four and five hours took sixteen and the only food or drink you could get was from stalls set up at stations by the Women's Volunteer Service. As soon as the train pulled in at a station there was a concerted rush and the ladies, bless them, performed magnificently. Hot strong tea and a sausage roll or sandwich tasted like nectar and ambrosia when I managed to get it.

On arrival at Edinburgh I contacted the military Transport office to find out about the next leg of my journey. The train for Rosyth left an hour later and I was onboard and this time had a seat well before the train left. This train passes through many small villages of great historical interest but the most interesting part is the passage over the Forth Bridge. A magnificent structure over the river Forth and from which can be seen the broad stretch of the river with the island of Inchkeith in the distance. If I were asked how many times after that first time I have passed either over or under that bridge I could not possibly say, too many would be my reply.

On arrival at Rosyth station many sailors disembarked and I saw a couple of Navy transports waiting outside the gate. There was a WREN driver in each of them and I asked what their destination was. The routine they told me was to pick up all the passengers and, if the ship they were going to was in harbour they would take them into the dockyard to the ship. If the ship was not there they took them to a large depot ship where they were berthed until their ship arrived. The Wallace, according to them was in harbour so I climbed into the transport.

Here I must digress. The Wallace was one of 3 destroyers built between 1917 and 1924 and were classed as the Shakespeare class. They were intended to act as destroyer leaders to the V and W class destroyers, which were completed in the latter half of World War One. Four of the V and W served with the Royal Australian Navy and the remainder with the Royal Navy. They were called the V and W class because their names commenced with either V or W. They were armed for the type of war that no longer existed namely low angle guns and torpedo tubes.

They were small as modern destroyers go being only 1090 to 1120 tons but they had four conventional boilers that gave them a speed up to 33 knots, which was faster than the modern Hunt class escorts that were reclassified as destroyers when they entered the service in 1940. Fifteen of the V and W's were converted to escort vessels by the removal of torpedo tubes and changing their guns to 4.4 inch High angle Guns. They were outfitted with oerlikon guns 4-barrelled .5 machine guns two Lewis guns and later, as they became available, Bofors guns.

Anti Submarine equipment (ASDIC) was added and additional depth charges and later depth charge throwers. Eventually RADAR was added, first known as RDF (radio direction finding). The additional equipment had, of course to be manned and the addition of men to carry out these duties resulted in crowded living conditions that were truly appalling. There was insufficient room to swing hammocks so men off watch had to sleep on the wooden tables, benches and the top of the lockers, which did double duty as seats.

Naturally it was impossible to spread out mattresses or blankets so they slept fully clothed even to their sea boots. Their outer garments would, on most occasions, be wet and the atmosphere in the mess, with all portholes closed, as was always the case at sea, the smell of food, the smoke from cigarettes and the ever-present odour of diesel oil is indescribable. Add to this a rough sea with water swilling from side to side under their feet as men clung onto anything handy to hold themselves in position and with new arrivals sea sick and vomiting before they could reach the upper deck and you have a living hell.

None of these ships had adequate capacity for drinking water and the distilling equipment could not cope with the long stretches at sea that convoy and wartime work demanded. They could not carry fresh vegetables for longer (in the case of Wallace) than four days. Cold storage for meat was restricted to four days. They carried one man designated as a cook, I say designated because his cooking capability was usually restricted to being able to boil water and make cocoa. The men had to prepare all their own food and take it to the galley with a wooden label attached which gave the cook directions on what the dish was supposed to be. His job was to cook it accordingly but the results would make a grown man weep if he had that emotional outlet but he didn't. Food was a major problem due to two factors. The total inadequacy of storage facilities and the system of canteen messing that I have previously described.

The officers were far better of from the point of view of accommodation This was not a deliberate act to favour them but simply a matter of design. The ship needed only the same number of officers as it's original design called for and therefore there was adequate cabin space with proper bunks and a small wardroom. The Captain also had a small sea cabin directly under the bridge. Most Captains were fully aware of the indescribable conditions in which the ship's company were living in and tried in many ways to alleviate it, always conscious of that thin borderline between discontent and mutiny.

Some day some one should tell the story of the V and W destroyers. Their record in action against modern ships where they were outgunned and under equipped in every way was truly magnificent. When used as Atlantic convoy and other convoy escorts they distinguished themselves and were the equal of any and better than most. The Viscount (one of them) celebrated her silver anniversary at sea by sinking a U Boat in the Atlantic on that day. These ships suffered a terrible toll and not many finished the war but it can be said that the Royal Navy would have been in difficult straits without them from the very beginning of the war.

The transport arrived alongside the Wallace. I will never forget my first sight of her on that January day in 1941 It was raining slightly, "scot's mist" they called it and everything was grey and uninviting. She was lying alongside the timber jetty in Rosyth, a jetty that was a hold over from sailing ship days. The combination of an ancient jetty and a destroyer that except for its armament was reminiscent of a bygone Navy filled me full of foreboding. I walked over the gangway to be met with great enthusiasm by the ship's Coxswain. I realised, on better acquaintance that this Chief represented everything good, not only about the ship but about the Navy in general. He was a Devonshire man and if the war had not started he would have been retired. He was rotund with a fresh complexion and a marked accent of Devon in his speech. Whenever I see a Santa Claus I think of him, without the beard of course.

I am afraid I didn't respond to his enthusiasm too well and almost the first thing I said was that I was only here temporarily. I said this because, before leaving the Signal School a casual comment was made that I overheard. This comment was that I would not be out of the School very long. I, mistakenly, thought they meant I was here temporarily, its real meaning became clear very quickly.

The Coxswain did not reply to my comment, he just grinned and said welcome onboard. He called two interested bystanders to take my kit down to the Chief and Petty Officers mess then he said the Captain was in his cabin aft and wanted to see me as soon as I came onboard. I made my way aft accompanied by the Coxswain (who, incidentally, is the most senior man on the lower deck) to the Captain's cabin. He had one cabin aft for use in harbour and a tiny cramped space of a sea cabin directly under the bridge. The Captain thanked him and indicated he wanted to see me alone. The Coxswain left and just for a few moments we studied each other.

He was a Lieutenant Commander who had left the navy before the war started. His family name was extremely well known and their connection to the Royal Family was such that their weddings, funerals, and baptisms usually had someone to represent the Royal Family in attendance. Naturally I did not know any of this at the time and was busy studying his appearance. He was a tall man, over six feet with a head of black wavy hair and quite good-looking. He smiled and I relaxed. I sensed immediately that our inevitable closeness would not be a strain as it so easily could be under the circumstances.

"They told me you were rather young," he said "But I must admit I never expected someone who looked like a school boy." The way he said it with a smile took away any resentment. I learned very quickly that I had had three predecessors in quick succession. Two of them had come in from being retired for several years and one had achieved his position in the reserves with absolutely no experience. With a Captain who had served continuously this might have been acceptable as the Captain would be up to date on the Signal books and the Conduct of the Fleet manuals but even so it would have been difficult.

With a Captain who had been totally out of touch for several years it was vital that the Yeoman knew his job fully. I learned that my predecessors were (through no fault of their own) for the most part totally ignorant of, not only modern manoeuvres but could not recognise the signals for what they were when they were received. Apparently, when in company with other destroyers, several mistakes had been made for which, of course, the Captain had been held responsible. They had not been dangerous mistakes but bad enough to get him very angry. When he requested replacements they had gone, according to the stories, from bad to worse.

Finally he had used his social contacts in the navy and demanded a proper replacement. I believe to this day that someone had become really angry with him for putting on pressure from above and due to his complaints of out of date people decided to send me. I think they thought I would be the horrible example. After a few words of welcome he told me to go forward and sling my hammock, we were sailing at first light.

We were heading down the Firth of Forth and passing under the Forth Bridge as a train went clacketing over the bridge. I later learned that the ship's company looked on this as a good omen; Seamen have a tendency to be superstitious. I felt the ship lift slightly to the swell, a not unpleasant feeling with very little roll. I found from experience that this destroyer had been superbly designed for her task. In the fiercest of storms when the bows were totally submerged as she plowed into a head sea and from the bridge nothing could be seen but the forward turret I learned to have total faith the bows would rise and shake off the tons of water and plunge on to meet the next wave.

As we went down towards the sea at a modest ten knots passing Inchkieth on our starboard side and Largo on our port side I read for the first time the convoy operational order. This defined who the escorts would be; two destroyers of which we were the senior escort; and the number of ships to be picked up at each port on the east coast. Which of the ships would have the convoy commodore onboard and what the ships were carrying. The speed of the convoy was laid down as seven and a half knots, deadly slow; but the speed of the convoy was dictated by the speed of the slowest ship. The distance from Methil to the Thames meant that three and a half days would be good timing. After spending a night at anchor in the Thames we then had a return, convoy the make up of which would be passed to us in London.

It all seemed straightforward and uncomplicated and I felt confident I could handle this routine with very little worry. Little did I know that I was entering into, what has since been referred to as, the most consistently hazardous convoy run ever experienced. When the run to Murmansk is taken into consideration and the Malta convoys are included this seems to be a gross exaggeration, but it isn't. The reason is the fact that each of these deadly convoys had a beginning and a definable end. The east coast convoys were constant, day after day, week after week, year after year and when a day passed without an attack by the enemy it was an exception. In addition every type of enemy aircraft could be and was used. Surface attacks by E Boats (German torpedo boats) was standard and on the occasions when we passed the Thames to pick up ships from a Channel convoy to join our northbound convoy, we had the guns of Cap Gris Nez to contend with.

The ships waiting to join the convoy were laying off Methil and we circled among them counting them and ticking them off on my list. The Captain had himself briefed me on what was required when we met the ships. The convoy commodore was flying his distinguishing flag and we hailed him on the loud hailer and exchanged greetings. The convoy slowly formed up in two columns and we went ahead with the other escort taking up position on the seaward quarter of the port column. There were 24 ships with cargoes of everything from gasoline to beer. It all seemed so smooth and well organised. As we left the Firth of Forth, May Island came into view and for some reason that, to me, in the future, seemed to signal the beginning and the end, a sight full of foreboding on the way out and a signal of safe harbour on our return.

The convoy had barely edged itself into two columns when a lookout called, "Aircraft overhead". All binoculars were raised and the aircraft could be seen dead ahead but extremely high. It was a German Dornier of the type generally referred to as a "Flying pencil". They were used a great deal as reconnaissance aircraft and this was obviously his duty. The ominous message was that the enemy now knew exactly when we had sailed and the total make up of the convoy. He was too high and far away to take a shot at, in any case our ammunition was too precious to use on something that was not an active threat to the convoy. We turned south and formed up in a straggly but reasonable two columns.

I then learned that the other destroyer acting as escort was new to this coast and this type of convoy; in fact it had only just finished its acceptance trials and had never fired a gun in anger. Prior to sailing our Captain had briefed the other Captain on what to expect, more or less, it was impossible to cover every contingency. Future events proved vividly the benefit of experience, or, if not experience the advice of someone who had been through it all before, unless of course, as in this case, the advice was totally ignored.

We plodded on with a following sea making it difficult for the ships to maintain a good line ahead. It is easier to keep a steady course when you are pushing into the sea rather than being carried forward. We had sailed early and the January chill was penetrating and uncomfortable but the Captain made no move to leave the bridge. I settled in my corner as best I could and a nudge at my arm made me turn to see one of the mess men with a steaming cup of hot cocoa, I could have blessed him. The cocoa was the Coxswain's doing, I found out later, he was determined that I would get every support he could offer and without it that first trip would have been an impossible to take experience instead of just being the nightmare it was.

At first I found it difficult to understand why, in what was obviously a period of calm, the Captain did not retire to rest in his sea cabin. This of course would have let me get down into the warmth of the wheelhouse at least. I soon found out that the Captain and the First Lieutenant were the only two officers onboard who could be trusted alone on the bridge. The other officers, of which there were five, were ninety-day wonders. These were men who had been selected for the ninety-day training programme to become sub lieutenants because they had a university degree of some sort.

The fact that their peace time employment had been tellers in banks or used car salesmen or as in one case a man who travelled the country selling balloons at fairs did not seem to be taken into consideration. Above all their selection did not take into account their intelligence in fundamental things, which in many cases was totally lacking. The majority of them were good people and I admired their fortitude in being pulled out of a calm existence to be subjected to life in a destroyer and when the danger was added to this total unfamiliarity I wondered if I could have endured such a change. But some of them were walking disasters to whom the idea of being an officer had gone to their heads. The courtesy of the service, the respect that normally flowed between officer and man in the navy, the method of addressing Chief and Petty Officers seemed to them to take away their new found elevated station and as a result they violated the very rules that would have helped them.

It is standard practice in the Royal Navy for officers to address each other by their last names, never their Christian names. The Captain of course, irrespective of rank, is addressed as such, except by authorities outside the ship; when he was then referred to by the name of his ship. The other officer, such as the First Lieut. (the next senior officer to the Captain), is referred to by his position or as number One. Any of the other officers holding special appointments such as Gunnery officer would be referred to as "Guns".

There is however a great deal of subtlety to all this in knowing when one officer should call another by his position or his last name. These practices and courtesies are as old as the navy itself. One practice is inviolate, an officer irrespective of his rank must never address a Chief or Petty Officer by his last name without preceding it by his rank. In a ship this can be shortened to just Chief or P.O. between officers of the ship and their men. This led to my first encounter with a Sub Lieut. who, for a short time, was the bane of my existence.

I was propped in the corner above my hooded table when I heard my last name called. I ignored it and continued to look through my binoculars at a passing ship. My name was repeated again, this time very loudly and I saw the Captain stir in his seat and glance over. I still ignored the call and suddenly I felt my shoulder shaken. I couldn't believe it. I turned with the binoculars raised in my hand, I didn't intend to hit him with them but it must have seemed to the Captain as if I was. "Yeoman", he called and I looked over. The Sub Lieut. had stepped back white in the face. "What was the name of the ship over there," "The Fulham 2 sir", I replied. He then turned to the Sub Lieut. and said, "Did you want something, Smith?" The Sub Lieut. looked at me, then at the Captain, "No Sir, I wanted to speak to the Yeoman." "It is very simple," said the Captain, "All you have to do is address him properly and he will answer, now leave the Bridge." I knew I had made an enemy but I had been in the Navy long enough to know that the man who never made an enemy, never made a friend.

The convoy was making its steady way when St. Abbs Head came into view and suddenly all hell broke loose. The cloud level was thick and high and we had no hint, not even the sound of engines that aircraft were about. This of course was well before the days when ship's had radar or RDF as we at first called it. The first we knew was that unearthly scream of falling bombs followed by a huge mountain of water ahead of the convoy. The bell was sounded for action stations and within a matter of less than three minutes every man was at his action station, the guns were swinging round following the Director and every eye was turned to the sky. The convoy plodded along as if nothing had happened and we neither increased speed nor altered course. Another tremendous scream and the water about 600 yards to port of us erupted in awful fury. We still couldn't see anything to shoot at and the feeling is, to say the least, frustrating.

There was a cry from the lookout although we must have all seen them at once. Four heavy bombers passed through a small area of broken cloud then vanished again. The waiting is nerve wracking and far worse than being able to fight back. Time passed and it became clear they had done their bombing runs and gone home. We stood down from action stations and I realised I was very hungry.

The Captain was talking to the First Lieut., "They came a little earlier today number One," "Yes sir, I thought I would have time to eat but I didn't make it." I suddenly realised that what I had witnessed was not an isolated attack but an established routine of this convoy run.

The Captain left the bridge for his sea cabin so I went down to the mess where I cornered the Coxswain and for the first time could get some answers. I learned that the attack I had just witnessed was merely the beginning of a pattern. The enemy knew exactly where we were and how fast we were travelling. Depending on the weather and using well known land marks he could attack us at will and select the best type of aircraft or weapon for the attack.

Knowing this we could ourselves make some predictions such as when was the best time to try and eat. This meant that the ship was constantly at stand by action stations with a few men at every position day and night in all weathers. It also meant that we would be at full action stations at dawn and dusk plus those times when the enemy had made a habit of attacking. In effect we were in the front line week after week, month after month and as it turned out, year after year.

The attacks came regularly, next Holy Island then when dropping off and picking up ships coming out of the Tyne. Flamborough Head seemed to be a popular spot for them as it was usually quite rough around there and the convoy had a tendency to bunch up a little. From an aircraft point of view the worst was Hull and south of there. This is where the Stuka 87's had their fun. These were dive-bombers and would come over in groups of eight. Their tactics were to line up in single line at one end of the convoy then slip individually following each other into a mind numbing screaming attack, releasing their bomb and then pulling out.

Our Captain had warned our new escort about this type of attack and told him that he should open fire with a barrage the moment they were sighted. This demoralised them as they couldn't line up and play follow my leader and as a result, their practised bombing attacks were disrupted and they became quite inaccurate. On this day the first approach was made to the port quarter of the convoy where the other escort was stationed.

We watched them approach while of course watching for any other group. We had increased speed to clear the way for our guns and I could hear the Captain saying aloud as if he could talk to the other Captain, "Open fire, for God's sake open fire," As we moved clear so that our guns could bear the aircraft got into their bombing line and still there was no firing.

As we opened fire with a barrage the other escort opened fire, he had fallen into the trap of thinking that they would be easier to hit when lined up. The second bomb hit him just aft of the funnel then the nearest merchantman was hit. Our guns had swung away to line up on the second wave approaching from ahead. There was no hesitation and a barrage of shells as fast as they could be loaded and fired was put up between the aircraft and the convoy. The sky literally turned a solid black between them and us, and it would have been suicide for them to try and pass through it. They turned away and jettisoned their bombs; this was standard practice for them to lighten their load to stretch their limited resources of fuel.

When it was obvious the attack was over, at least for a time, we called the other ship for a damage report. She reported severe structural damage but was seaworthy and could make into the nearest harbour under her own steam. I do not know how many men were killed and injured in this attack but I do know that if advice had been taken it could possibly have been avoided. An ironic twist to this was that just before vanishing round the headland to enter harbour she called by light with a religious quotation. We always carried a bible and a book of common prayer as well as books of quotations on the bridge as this method of exchanging comments was universal in the R.N. The quotation when found said, "Here endeth the first lesson." We were not amused.

The merchantman had suffered no casualties as the bomb had exploded on hitting the sea alongside. She was holed but they had contained the damage and could go in at their own power. We circled her and waved, the incredible bravery of these unarmed merchantmen has never been truly acknowledged and they waved back as if going on holiday.

CHAPTER TWELVE

E-Boat Alley

I had lost track of time. I had eaten and slept in a blur of tension, always wondering what was coming next. The idea of taking off and changing my clothes let alone having a bath was ridiculous. The toilets were cupboard like steel boxes just inside the port waist of the ship so they could be accessed by going down the port ladder from the bridge within seconds. Even then there was a reluctance to be absent from the bridge for sufficient time to use them. Of course we had to but it always seemed to me that the action bell went just as I got there, probably an exaggeration because of my state of mind on this first trip.

The Coxswain, with his years of experience, knew my situation and sandwiches and hot cocoa arrived at and between mealtimes with heart-warming regularity. Every man on that ship owed him a debt of gratitude. He made sure that, even at almost constant action stations, the men manning the guns received hot cocoa from the galley and sandwiches at meal times. I know he made the cook's life very difficult and every spare body, and there wasn't many of those, were pulled into his support group as needed. He did all this by the sheer force of his personality from his action station position in the wheelhouse.

Here I would like to digress into the future a little, as the routine I have just described was responsible for this incident. As the war wore on we were sometimes asked to take military men from other countries for experience, I am sure they never forgot it. In this case it was a Colonel from the U.S. Army, a most charming individual with a pronounced New England accent. A routine had been established by the mess men to bake potatoes in their jackets, that is when we could get them. Around two in the morning one of them would come up on to the bridge to where I was propped in my corner leaning on the hooded table. Naturally it was usually pitch black, so the first I knew would be a push in the back. I would turn around and stick out my hands, which were of course heavily gloved with leather fronts. He would dump the potatoes in my hand and, with a whispered exchange, would leave. I would pop them in the hooded table and, with my gloves, tear them apart and eat them. No salt, no butter but to this day I have never tasted a baked potato any better. The Colonel had asked permission from the Captain to watch proceedings from the bridge and, of course, this had been granted. We had not anticipated however that, for his own reasons, sea sickness, claustrophobia or whatever, he would be on the bridge all night. In my absence he had taken over my normal position leaving me to walk up and down or prop up anywhere I could find.

Out of courtesy I could not ask him to move and I hoped the Captain would leave the bridge so I could get somewhere more comfortable. My eyes were naturally used to the dark and, what appeared to be pitch black to someone coming from down below, was quite visible to me. I was at the other side of the bridge when the mess man came up. He was immediately behind the Colonel and nudged him in the back. The Colonel turned and the mess man told him to stick out his hands. He did, no gloves, his howl split the silence and the mess man vanished down the ladder. The Captain, who had not observed the by-play, asked what happened. The Colonel, very upset, said, "I am obviously not very popular, someone stuck hot coals in my hands." I was busily looking around the deck for my potatoes, which I retrieved and popped in the hooded table. Then of course I had to explain in order to correct the awful impression the Colonel had received. I showed him the potatoes and he was totally convinced. He then apologised for taking up my space and for the rest of the trip he was never in the way. He did however take advantage of his knowledge and would appear within seconds of the mess man to share the potatoes on succeeding nights.

We were now approaching a stretch of water that became notorious as E Boat Alley. It was that area of water that lay off the coastline where "The Wash" was situated and extended down past Great Yarmouth to the Thames. The navigable channel in this area was very narrow. The route passed between the coast and the many sandbanks that in low water could be seen on our port side. The distance between the columns of the convoys had to be reduced and there was very little sea room for us to protect them to seaward. The German motor torpedo boats, or E Boats, as they were called were stationed in Holland and would start out in daylight to arrive at our position some time after dark. Their attack would come either when the night was overcast or the moon was mostly hidden but the largest attacks came when there was no moon. The reason for this was that our reconnaissance aircraft would see a large number of them if visibility were reasonable. So at these times the attacking force would be four or six of them that had separated for the journey across and met at an agreed rendezvous point. On one occasion about which I will elaborate later we were attacked by forty-four of them.

On this occasion we were warned by the shore-ship radio that a group of four or six had been seen leaving Holland. Needless to say we were at full action stations, with the forward gun loaded with star shell and everyone in the ship listening for the sound of engines. In the light of today's advances in Radar, this seems like an awfully crude way of detecting the enemy, it was the only one we had.

It started, as I found out it usually started, with the awful crump of an explosion. You have to experience this to appreciate exactly the horror of it. At the same time as the explosion, the deck under your feet would bang and vibrate as the sound waves hit the ship. The immediate order was given to open fire in the direction of the explosion with starshell. The night turned into day as the forward gun reloaded and fired star shell. I could see through the binoculars the speeding bow wave of an E Boat as it left the scene and called its range and bearing to the director. They swung on to it and the sea around it erupted in massive explosions. All hell had broken loose and every gun was bearing on its target of opportunity. The oerlikons were firing from each sponson, the point five machine guns were creating that terrible tearing sound and the four-inch pounded away creating a wave of explosions that it seemed nothing could live through.

We had increased speed and were now placing ourselves between the convoy and the attacking force. The guns on our port side could no longer bear safely due to the proximity of the convoy but the constant hammer of those guns that could bear beat through my eardrums and, for a moment I felt like standing there doing nothing but cover my ears. The feeling passed and I concentrated on passing ranges and bearings of anything I sighted that was not being engaged and sure enough one of the guns would swing round so it wouldn't feel neglected.

The ship that had been hit was on fire and listing badly. As we passed they were abandoning ship by jumping over the side and also trying to launch life rafts and a lifeboat. I saw the lifeboat fall uselessly from one of its davits and hang there in an impossible position. An E Boat was on fire having been hit with the Oerlikon shells and we could see the heavy stern wake of others as they retreated. They would probably reform and attack again according to the Captain, so there was no chance of returning to pick up survivors until that danger had passed. We turned south again and stayed at the seaward side, our damaged escort had not been replaced so we were strictly on our own.

The order was given to fire star shell to seaward at staggered intervals and when this happened every eye in the ship would search the visible area. After a time this had to be stopped, our ammunition was limited. Well over an hour had passed. The stricken ship had sunk leaving the survivors in their life jackets or clinging to what debris they could and we could do nothing about it without jeopardising the whole convoy. The Commodore had passed a message to a merchant ship asking him to try and pick up survivors but a stopped ship was an inviting target and, as the convoy had moved on leaving the survivors behind, it was impossible until all danger of attack had gone to try and pick them up.

The next attack came from behind but fortunately one of the lookouts spotted the bow waves coming up between us and almost up to the convoy. The director turned the rear guns on to the target and opened fire almost before the lookout had time to finish his report. We turned to port to bring all guns to bear and once again the night turned hideous with sound. They turned away but this time we had three of them in clear view and at close range and the Oerlikons and point five's ripped into them. One burst into flames then blew up with a resounding roar. There were no survivors from the E Boats. We rejoined the convoy and stayed close to the survivors of the merchant ship while a small tug that had been in the convoy picked up any he could find. The rest of the night passed without incident and at dawn we turned to count the number of ships that were still in formation. One of course was a casualty but fortunately there had been no stragglers and the convoy was still reasonably intact.

On my convoy list I had the names of the ships bound for the Thames and these would be escorted until they could make their own way up the river to whatever dock they were destined for. We entered the mouth of the Thames with almost a sigh of relief but I don't know why, because the regular visits of mine laying aircraft and the constant threat of high level bombing didn't exactly make it a safe haven. As we were turning in to approach the boom vessel to enter the main harbour the radio room called me on the voice pipe to haul up a message. The messages were placed in a tube at the end of a long piece of cod line and had to be hauled up by hand. At the same time the boom vessel flashed a signal telling us to stand by outside the boom.

The message had been received on the broadcast. Direct ship to ship, with the appropriate answering system, would have betrayed both our position and our identity to the enemy. I must admit I thought this a bit ironic, as the enemy knew where we were every step of the way. As an overall policy however it made a lot of sense. The message was encrypted and the duty to put in to plain language normally fell on a designated officer. This was a good idea because the messages could contain anything from operational orders to highly secret information for the Captain only. By restricting its' contents onboard to one designated person, any leak could be easily contained.

This was the first one received, so I was totally in the dark as I was about many things on this first trip. As my predecessor had left before I arrived, I was literally groping for answers that should have been supplied in detailed hand over discussions and notes. I asked the Officer of the Watch (O.O.W.) who was a pleasant young sub, who was the designated cypher officer. It turned out to be Smith with whom I had already had a run in and, during the trip, had never spoken to me once since the first incident. Instead, he had spoken to the signalmen when he had a query about the convoy and the signalman had asked me and relayed the information. This was even when he was standing near enough to touch me on the bridge. It was pathetically childish.

I gave the message to the boatswain's mate who was always standing by at the back of the bridge to carry out any type of duty that the bridge personnel required. I sent him to Smith with the message and told him to call attention to the fact it had a high priority. There is a very high tide in the Thames area and when the tide is receding the river flow to the sea can be as high as 7 knots. Keeping a destroyer in position, particularly when ships are moving in and out of the fairway is no easy task. The Captain had decided to circle in a small area below the boom but occasionally we had to go bows on to the tide and steam ahead to maintain our position. I describe this because it illustrates the difficult and frustrating task of waiting to find out what the orders were.

Some time passed, more than adequate to decypher the message, but there was no information forthcoming. The Captain called down the voicepipe to tell the messenger to get Sub Lieut. Smith and ask him to report to the bridge. He arrived in a rush with the message still gripped in his hand. He was asked what the contents were and he replied that he couldn't decypher the message and he had consulted the other officers and they said they couldn't help him. The Captain was furious, he had been juggling the ship for nearly half an hour to be faced with this. "Do you know which particular cypher it is in," he asked. This was a reasonable question, we carried several methods of encryption, some relying on one book, some cross referencing to another book and some relying on a one time pad or stencil cypher. By experience it was possible to glance at the encrypted version and recognise the method most likely to have been used. "No sir," "Then did you ask the Yeoman?" Smith turned and looked at me then back at the Captain, "No sir, I understood that I was the cypher officer."

It was a difficult time, how can you explain the workings of the Navy in a short sentence. How can you tell an officer, full of his newly found authority and dignity that, by putting a label on a jar you don't change the contents? The Captain, angry as he was, restrained himself and quietly told me to go below with Smith to assist in decrypting the message. Smith was furious and, when we reached the cabin where the books were kept, he made this quite clear by his comments. I kept my temper and explained to him as tactfully as I could that part of my job was deeply involved in all codes and cyphers used by the Navy.

This was no loss of face to anyone and it was usual for the designated cypher officer who had not had the benefit of any course to ask the Yeoman what system the message was in then take it from there. We decrypted the message in a very few minutes and it was our orders for picking up a few ships from a channel convoy and bringing them round to rendezvous with the north bound convoy the following day. I shuddered to see that the rendezvous point was off Dover.

On return to the bridge with the message the Captain pointed us out to sea and we proceeded out into the estuary. Again I did not have any idea whether this was a regular routine or an occasional one. If either of these then everyone, particularly the Captain would be fully aware of the Cape Gris Nez guns. If it was a new experience then, as had happened to me before, I did not want it to come as a deadly surprise. The Captain was no fool, "What's bothering you Yeoman," he asked. "The guns sir," I replied. "What guns," he queried. "The Cape Griz Nez guns," "What about them," I realised that this was indeed a first and everyone in authority had taken it for granted, as they did so many times to everyone's detriment, that we were aware of the dangers and would act appropriately. I told him about my experiences with the Channel convoys, the constant bombardment once you entered the target area and the necessity from the moment you entered for everyone normally exposed on the upper deck to be either stationed below or, if not possible, to be instructed to take cover when the alarm bell was pushed instead of rushing to action stations. We never wore steel helmets and in fact they were never on the bridge but under these circumstances steel helmets were essential.

The Captain sent for the First Lieut. and all the other officers. He made no reference to our conversation but briefed them in detail on what to expect and what to convey to the ship's company as if he had been fully familiar with the coming problem. I was really pleased with this approach, as it placed the responsibility exactly where it should be and also kept faith with the ship's company's belief in his extreme competence. We steered out into the channel and increased speed in order to make the rendezvous point before dark. Despite my forebodings we passed through the target area without incident. We were of course moving at more than three times the speed of a convoy, in addition the Germans rarely fired at a single ship as accurate firing was impossible but into a group of ships the chance of hitting was greatly enhanced.

We met the convoy just before dark; there were only four ships and their escort of one Hunt class destroyer and a trawler towing a barrage balloon to discourage low level attacks. We exchanged the usual courtesies and received by light the names, destinations and cargoes of our new charges and the escorts turned back. Where they were going and what was their next duty was none of our business.

We pulled almost alongside the ship who had been designated Commodore and, by loud hailer, introduced ourselves and asked if they had any problems, the answer was no so we stationed ourselves ahead and to seaward and settled down to the slow speed of the convoy. We steamed without incident for almost two hours when the officer responsible for navigating spoke up from the hooded table to tell the Captain that we would be in the danger zone in about 15 minutes.

The news was passed round the ship and the steel helmets that had been brought up to the bridge were put on. I always felt ridiculous in a steel helmet and throughout the war very rarely had occasion to wear one like most other small ship people. It was a pitch-black night and I had my binoculars pointed across the strait to where I thought the first flash would come and I almost missed it. A very faint blossom of flame that almost seemed a figment of the imagination flickered in the corner of my left eye. "Opened fire," I practically screamed and the alarm bell pushed by the Captain resounded throughout the ship.

No one else had seen the flash for the simple reason they did not know what they were actually expecting to see. I had seen that flicker too many times not to recognise it, but I must admit that in the just over 60 seconds it took the shells to land I wondered if I had given a false alarm. We used to count to ourselves, ticking off the seconds by counting in our heads, one crocodile, two crocodile etc, try it I think you will find it pretty accurate. At the count of fifty I laid flat on the deck and I must admit that for the first time I had mixed feelings on whether I was hoping I was right or wrong.

All the bridge personnel followed suit and suddenly the sea erupted with an enormous roar. The crack of shrapnel falling harmlessly on the ship and then a delayed salvo landing, this time further away. A few seconds passed and we all stood up and I immediately went back to studying the distant coast with my binoculars. A few minutes went by and then there was an almost simultaneous cry from everyone watching the coast. I knew then they all had the message and we wouldn't miss any firing.

The salvos continued to land but except for shell fragments and shrapnel hitting the ships there was no damage. I had been counting the number of seconds from firing to exploding and it reached 72. I knew from experience that we were almost out of range and I said so. Sure enough that was the last salvo and we settled down for the rest of the trip. The Captain asked me how many times I had been through that particular experience and truthfully I told him I had lost count.

After the shelling stopped the night was quiet. We made our way towards the Thames, and like a sheepdog circling his flock we herded the ships along. We arrived at the entrance to the Thames after daylight as the other ships to make up the convoy to go north were assembling. The promise of a nights sleep at anchor or alongside vanished and we started our round up routine. The Pilot vessel came alongside with a packet, which was opened by the Captain on the bridge.

He handed me the list of ships, their destinations, and their cargo. This time there were 32 ships and again their cargo was greatly varied. Fortunately we rarely had any tankers carrying gasoline although we did get small coastal tankers carrying crude oil. We carried out our usual check and made our acquaintance with the Commodore.

I did not know what to expect on this first leg of the northbound journey. We were now heading for E boat alley in daytime and I knew they would never attack during the day. We had barely started to turn north when the leading ship of the starboard column practically disintegrated. She had struck a mine and the force of the explosion was incredible.

She sank within a few minutes and the survivors and debris were scattered over what seemed an impossibly large area. We closed in and dropped climbing nets over the side and members of our ship's company climbed down the nets and helped the struggling, oil-covered men to get on to the nets. We picked up 9 men out of a crew of 17, two of them died within minutes. We called a small tug over who was escorting the rear of the convoy until we cleared the area. Transferring the oil-covered men and the bodies was not easy but finally the tug headed back into harbour and we could get on with our escort duties.

The convoy had plodded steadily ahead so we increased speed and caught them up. We told the Commodore what had happened then settled down into our escort routine. The messages that had come out with the packet contained a navigational warning that aircraft were believed to have sewn mines in the entrance to the Thames and the sweepers had covered the area. Obviously they had missed at least one. It was late afternoon and the rest of the day passed without incident.

As usual we closed up for action station at dusk and just before dark received an enemy report of E Boats. They had been spotted by fighter aircraft on patrol and according to the report there were five of them. The lookout on the port side suddenly screamed E Boats and every gun turned towards the shore thinking they had sneaked inboard of us. I saw the fighting lights of the leading motor gunboat (MGB) as they tore towards the convoy. The fighting lights were three lights vertical, red, blue and white and the sequence was changed every eight hours. After a rapid check against the correct sequence they were declared friendly and the Captain gave the order to hold fire and the three of them passed ahead of us on the way to meet the reported E Boats.

We breathed a sigh of relief but it is a big ocean and without any means of detecting the enemy other than by sight or sound the chances of missing them so they could get through to the convoy was very high. We plodded on and suddenly from the seaward side I caught sight of s very small blue light making our pendants. It was the MGB's they had been unable to make contact with the enemy so were warning us they were patrolling near the convoy on our seaward side.

We acknowledged the signal and I must admit we felt somewhat relieved. It was almost midnight and we had reverted to stand by stations almost two hours when all hell broke loose. Our action bell went and the guns swung seeking a target. We could see streams of tracer low down over the water not more than a mile away. The tracer criss-crossed making it obvious that a battle was going on. The order was given to open fire with star shell and under it's light we could see the E Boats and the MGB's racing around trying to get the better of each other.

When the star shell started to descend we could see that some of the boats had detached and were heading away at high speed. These were obviously the E Boats who certainly did not want to hang around when faced with a vastly superior force now we had joined in. The three MGB's headed towards us so we were safe in firing salvoes after the retreating enemy. I don't think we hit any, but an MGB closed and on the loud hailer exchanged pleasantries such as, "we couldn't hit fish in a barrel" etc., etc. They headed back in towards the coast and we resumed our plodding way up the coast after standing down from action stations.

CHAPTER THIRTEEN

The Battle Of Britain

We arrived back at the Thames Estuary to find the enemy had been quite busy during the night laying mines from aircraft. Our entrance was protected by wooden minesweepers going ahead of us. The occasional boom of an exploding mine triggered by their magnetic sweeps kept us on edge then the look out reported a floating mine dead ahead. The minesweeper was also sweeping with the conventional paravane system that cut mines loose. This was one of the moored mine type and the minesweeper was frantically signalling to make sure we had seen the mine. We hoisted the alarm signal to alert the ships following us then opened fire with the oerlikon to explode the mine.

The man on the gun fired two rounds in rapid succession and they obviously hit the mine. It is difficult to describe the force of the explosion that is generated from an object that looked so small. The concussion from the explosion could be felt almost as a physical blow although we were at a considerable distance. It created a water spout that seemed at least fifty feet high and the water for hundreds of yards around shuddered in violent circles. We hauled down the alarm and proceeded to our anchorage while the ships passed us and made their way into the Port of London.

We stayed at anchor and everyone took advantage of attending to their personal needs with a bath high on the list. The Chief and P.O.s had a bathroom that could, at a pinch, hold four people under two showers. The men had a bathroom that could accommodate only six so many of them stripped and rigged a shower on the upper deck. This of course was cold water and they did not stay out there for long. Later the fresh water was cut off due to shortage of drinking water and bathing was done in salt water. This is an awful experience as it is impossible to get a lather and even after drying you never really feel clean. The lack of fresh water was one of the most difficult shortages to bear. The ships own distillation plant could not keep pace with the demand and later, when we moved into hot climates the situation was critical.

We anchored in or near this berth in the Thames during convoy changeover. It was from here in the Fernie I had watched the masses of German aircraft passing over in broad daylight to attack London. I had a front row seat in what became to be known as "The Battle of Britain", and watched the "So few" as Churchill called them, plough into the massed bombers and scatter them all over the sky. From my vantage point it seemed as if many of the bombers kept to their course for London while all around them the fighters shot their companions down and battled with their fighter escort. I could hear the crump of bombs falling on London and the men onboard whose families lived in London were bundles of anxious tension. Six months had passed but to me it was like yesterday.

The news of the war we were receiving at this time was certainly not good and as we ploughed our way out to pick up another convoy, for the first time, there was not much to keep our spirits up. When this kind of a mood starts to permeate a ship every little annoyance becomes a major grievance and in the confines of a ship where discomfort is the normal order of the day every grumble is magnified into a major complaint. We had some difficulty keeping both members of our own staff and other members of the ship's company from outright fights.

When this occurs a major diversion is needed. This diversion can be anything from getting a good meal for a change or finding something on which all the pent up anger can be expressed. It was the latter situation that occurred.

The Admiralty had ordered constructed several dummy ships that, from the air, looked like warships and in one case an aircraft carrier. These ships were old merchant ships and had a skeleton crew to steam them as necessary. They would be assembled in some fleet anchorage to deceive the enemy into thinking there was a Royal Naval force in the harbour. We were passing through the extremely shallow water off the south east coast when, to our absolute amazement, we saw the flight deck of a partially submerged aircraft carrier to seaward of us. We examined it closely through the binoculars and realised we were looking at one of the dummy ships.

Some absolute idiot had put the dummy in convoy down the east coast; the most dangerous run that could be imagined. Needless to say the enemy attacked that convoy day and night with everything they had until in these shallow waters they had been successful in sinking the ship. On many occasions I wondered who could possibly make decisions as stupid as this, as this was not an isolated case. I encountered several cases where it was obvious that either total ignorance of the conditions or total disregard of the risks had prevailed over common sense.

In this case it led to one of the most intensely fought skirmishes we were ever engaged in. It was almost dark and fortunately we were at night action stations. A lookout who had been examining the wreck in the fading daylight reported seeing movement. Immediately every binocular was turned on the protruding flight deck and emerging from hiding behind the wreck came E Boats. They had taken advantage of the shelter so generously provided for them and hidden waiting for the next convoy. They made the mistake of moving before it was properly dark and gave us at least a little warning.

We opened fire with starshell and could clearly see four of them spreading out and heading for the convoy. They were too close for our main armament to bear on them but our short-range weapons poured a stream of fire and the ships in the convoy that had light armament joined the fray. The sky seemed to be filled with tracer bullets like a fireworks display. We continued to illuminate the scene with starshell and turned to intercept them before they could get among the ships in the convoy, a trick they played whenever possible.

One of them turned towards us and passed up our starboard side pouring machine gun shells and cannon in our direction. Our oerlikon and point five's together with the Lewis Guns all swung on to this daring enemy who went into a surface action against a destroyer. He turned away but as he turned he exploded into a mass of flames and within seconds there was nothing to see but a patch of disturbed water. The intense fire combined with the lack of the surprise they had hoped for discouraged the others and they retreated without hitting one ship with their torpedoes. The Chief Stoker, due to lack of accommodation in the mess had made up a bunk in the workshop just aft of the funnel.

After the action when he went to turn in he found his workshop riddled with cannon fire from the E Boat and his nicely made bunk and his personal possessions full of rather large holes. The generator that acted as part of the emergency supply was totally wrecked but no one had been hurt. He repaired his bunk, made up a supply of wooden plugs which he hammered into the holes to make it watertight and for a time it looked like a porcupine house.

It is impossible to repeat in detail the actions that took place on the East Coast in the spring of 1941. In that spring the weather was really bad and on one occasion we were hove to off Flamborough Head for nearly three days. When it became obvious that the weather was going to make convoy work impossible we ordered the ships to enter harbour to wait out the storm. This they did except one extremely small flat top cargo ship. She couldn't have been more than three hundred tons and plied her trade in coastal waters around Britain.

The Captain signalled that he could not turn into a beam sea to enter harbour for fear of sinking; he was heavily loaded. As a result we stayed with him and for nearly three days we were abeam of Flamborough Head with the engines of the small vessel only able to keep her bows into the oncoming sea and not make any headway. Three days later we were still abeam of Flamborough. The wind dropped and the convoy emerged from it's shelter and formed up again.

We had during this period a respite from the bombers but the area in which we were reforming was the place where the dive-bombers made their regular appearance. The weather must have kept them away but we had hardly formed up in two columns when the lookout spotted aircraft approaching. Action stations were sounded and we prepared for the dive-bomber attack. There was, as usual, two formations of them and following their familiar routine flew towards the head and the stern of the convoy. The other escort was no amateur and started putting up a barrage just as we did.

With shells exploding all round them they pressed home their attack but they were prevented from lining up and diving one after the other on their chosen target. They were forced to carry out individual attacks on selected targets and met a barrage of small arms fire. As this was happening, with all our concentration on the dive-bombers, the sea all around us exploded with a stick of bombs. They had introduced a new tactic. While we were concentrating on the dive-bombers a group of JU88 high-level bombers had arrived unnoticed above us and were now dropping their bombs without anti aircraft fire to distract them. We were extremely fortunate that their aim was poor and none of the bombs made a direct hit. Two ships in the convoy reported superficial damage but no casualties.

We were now switching the after guns to the second target while maintaining our action with the dive-bombers. At that moment I must admit I did not like the situation one bit. Our ears were deafened by the gunfire but the scream of a lookout penetrated. He was pointing towards the shore and swinging round I saw four aircraft either Spitfires or Hurricanes, I could not distinguish which, approaching the convoy. Within seconds they were among the enemy and that sound of tearing canvas filled the air. We of course ceased firing as we could hit friendly aircraft.

The dive-bombers went into full retreat but I received the impression that the high level bombers were taken by complete surprise as first one then another burst into flames and headed smoking out to sea. The others, becoming aware of their danger, turned and headed for home with the fighters in hot pursuit. We breathed a prolonged sigh of relief but we had learned another lesson and ever after our lookouts were trained to ignore the ongoing battle and scan the skies for a surprise attack. The remainder of the trip back to the Forth was uneventful and it was with a sigh of relief we pulled into the Timber Jetty.

It was the middle of May and we were preparing, as usual, for our next convoy when we received orders to raise steam with all dispatch and prepare for sea. The Captain and First Lieutenant were called ashore for a briefing and when they returned we cast off and headed for the open sea.

At the entrance to the Forth we turned north and headed to go around the Pentland Firth into the Atlantic. When we were through we made a rendezvous with, what appeared to be, a miscellaneous collection of different types of destroyers. These were formed up by the leaders into a single line abreast that spread for miles, as the distance between ships was horizon distance. We were in the very right hand position and maintaining a speed of 25 knots.

The Captain then briefed the ship's company and the task force to which we had been attached was sweeping the Atlantic looking for the Bismarck. The battleships had sailed with their escorting destroyers Contact had been made by the Suffolk with the Bismarck and Prinz Eugen. From then on we were kept in the picture by intercepting the enemy reports generated by the Suffolk and Norfolk Meanwhile we were ordered to sweep towards the West in order to ensure the two German ships could not escape unseen back to Brest.

The story of the Bismarck and it's sinking does not need repetition but the signal that came in reporting the loss of the Hood with only three survivors shook us all. The next shake up was when the Bismarck was reported lost and for a time it looked as if, despite all our efforts, she was going to escape as the Prinz Eugen had done. The

R.A.F. Coastal Command flying Catalinas were patrolling the area from Iceland and on the 26th May, 30 hours after she had been lost, a patrolling Catalina found her and despite intense fire closed her to confirm her identity. Flying Officer D.A. Briggs of RAF 209 Squadron managed to send a report before losing contact. The reports being received were being broadcast around the ship by the Captain and the roar of approval that went up on this news was heartening. Her sinking followed shortly after and we were ordered to return to harbour.

Apparently U Boats had been ordered to converge in order to give support to the Bismarck and within four hours of turning for home ASDIC reported a contact. We were steaming independently so could call on no one to carry out the classic two destroyer attack where one keeps the target and the other depth charges and vice versa. The target was confirmed and we went into the attack. The men on the depth charges had all their work cut out for as fast as we completed one run we were circling and doing another depth charge attack. The men raced backwards and forwards between the depth charge rails setting the depth charges at the depth ordered by the Captain.

We were on the third run over the contact when something went wrong. The depth charges rolled over the stern and within seconds there was a massive explosion right under our stern. The men aft were thrown off their feet and on the bridge it had all the feeling of a torpedo explosion. One of the depth charges had exploded barely feet below the surface and the result was one of our screws was deformed out of useable shape and it appeared that the main shaft to the screws had been distorted.

With all engines stopped we wallowed in the water a perfect target for any U Boat. We were lucky and while the engine room staff examined the damage we kept an anxious but close watch all around us. The Captain was informed that the port screw was so badly damaged it could not be used but the starboard screw could still function. The engines were started and trailing a useless screw with the deck bouncing under our feet from some shaft imbalance we made slow progress towards the Clyde.

The days that passed until we reached harbour were among the most uncomfortable I have ever spent. For some reason the water supply had to be severely rationed; the bad weather that we encountered made cooking a hot meal impossible. For four and a half days we lived on tinned pilchards, on bread or corned beef, or for a change, cold tinned sausages. We couldn't wash or shave and the clothes we stood up in were kept on the whole time. We finally made harbour and tied up in Clydebank in mid afternoon of the fifth day. The ship was in a horrible state with the mess decks four inches deep in water with an oily scum over everything. She was totally uninhabitable so all sorts of transport came alongside and the ships company were dispersed among the citizens of Glasgow who had spare rooms. I was responsible for the confidential books etc that had to be taken for safe keeping to the nearest Naval Facility. As a result, I and the signalman I had kept behind to help, were the last to need billeting. The police car that took us to the Naval Facility with the books now took us to a Police Station in the centre of a residential district in Glasgow.

By this time it was late in the evening and quite dark. In the Police Station an Inspector was sitting behind a desk drinking tea. He looked up as we came in, then he groaned. "Not another two," he said. It transpired that he had the responsibility that day for billeting all the ship's company and he had been all over the area finding them accommodation. He told the driver of the police car that he would go with us and we were hustled back into the car.

We only travelled a couple of streets and pulled over outside a very imposing looking house. He consulted his pad of papers and said that a bedroom with two beds was registered as available by the compulsory billeting order. We mounted the steps and rang the bell. A maid came to the door and he, using the name of the owner, asked for her. She rang the bell. The landlady and her husband were out at the theatre so without more ado he ushered us into the hallway over the protests of the maid and told her to inform her mistress she had two people billeted on her. He then left.

The maid showed us through to the sitting room which was occupied by three men all doing their own thing. One was reading, another playing solitaire and another gently touching the piano keys as he followed a melody. We were seated on the settee by the maid, and incredibly not one of them even acknowledged our presence. Admittedly we must have looked a sorry state, unshaven with the clothes and duffel coats we had been wearing constantly for five days. But still, I felt that they must be aware of what we were and what we were doing and more importantly why we were there.

It was 9 p.m. and we were dog-tired and hungry. I asked the maid if she had anything we could eat and could we have a cup of tea. She seemed terrified at what her mistress was going to say when she found us there and she told us she could not give us anything. None of the men, although they clearly heard our request, made any comment. It was gone 11 and we could scarcely keep our eyes open when the mistress arrived with her husband and before she entered there was a whispered consultation in the hall with the maid.

I will never forget my first sight of that woman. She came sailing through into the sitting room, a stoutish woman about fifty years of age, dressed in a beautiful fur coat open at the front with a huge dangling necklace of about five strands of pearls. We stood up and she went right into the attack. "Get out of my house" she said, "This is a respectable house, not a flophouse for sailors." The young signalman turned red in the face with anger but I put up my hand and said "Come on", and headed for the door. I could not trust myself to speak or even look at her. Her husband stood behind her and I wished with all my heart that he had said what she said. I know I would have cheerfully assaulted him in his own home.

Outside we started to walk and the signalman asked where we were going. To find a Police Station I told him, they will make sure we get somewhere to sleep even if it is the cells. The dim blue light that shone over the police station steps was a welcome sight and we entered. The first person I saw standing behind a kind of lectern was the inspector who had billeted us. I told him what had happened and he was furious. He called a car around and we all got in and started off.

Naturally I was on unfamiliar ground so could not tell where we were headed and was horrified when we again pulled up at the same house. I protested adamantly that we did not want any part of these people. He ignored me and although by now it was after midnight he leaned on the bell. The door was opened by the mistress herself and he ushered us all into the hallway so the door could be closed to put the light on. Her husband arrived and she started to protest in a voice that was almost a scream.

The inspector put up his hand and she stopped squalling. "It is very simple," he told them. "Under the wartime billeting act you have been registered by the inspectors as having a spare room with two beds. I am empowered under this act to billet two servicemen here or, should you refuse, I can take you and your husband into custody. You will spend the night in cells and in the morning you can tell the magistrate why you defied the law."

"But" she said, "I expected that only officers would be selected to stay in my house." The look of disgust that came over the inspectors face was classical; he looked as if he had just tasted a very sour lemon. "You run a boarding house" he told her (this accounted for the men I had seen) "This is not a private mansion for the privileged few and may I remind you (and he almost shouted this) there is a war on and these men are fighting it". She finally agreed, much to my chagrin. I would much rather have seen her and her husband in cells and find somewhere else.

After the Inspector had left, she showed us our room. I must admit it was a really nice room and the beds turned out to be really comfortable. I asked her if, before turning in, we could have a bath. She said that we couldn't, as due to fuel rationing, the residents were only allowed one bath a week. On hearing this I started to put my coat back on. I turned and told the signalman to put his on we were leaving. She was furious, she knew where I would go and was afraid of the consequences. She gave in with ill grace and supplied towels etc. Despite the unpleasantness, that bath felt like sheer luxury; I could have slept in it.

We had carried with us an overnight bag with a set of underwear and a shaving kit. In the morning we had the luxury of a shave and a change of underwear but our outer garments were still slightly damp. In the common dining room we sat down for breakfast served by the maid. At another table the three men were having breakfast and didn't even glance at us when we entered. The breakfast arrived and it consisted of a piece of tinned tuna with a slice of bread and weak tea, there was neither butter nor margarine on our table. I felt this was the end of the road so I told the maid I wanted to see her mistress.

The mistress arrived full of bluster and ready for an argument. Before she could speak, I asked her why her other "lodgers" (I used the word deliberately) had a boiled egg, toast and butter etc. The word "lodger" took her out of her stride. "These are not lodgers, they are guests," she said. "Oh," I said, "They don't pay you then." "Of course they do," she said. "Where I come from, guests don't pay," I told her "Lodgers are people who pay and the place is called a Lodging House." I know that common usage for the sake of social face had turned lodgers into boarders and lodging houses into boarding houses but she was furious at my dragging away this protective social curtain. I then aired my complaint about the terrible breakfast we had been given. With an air of triumph she said, “You have no ration cards and food is short,” then with a sarcastic look she said, “There is a war on you know”.

CHAPTER FOURTEEN

Bed & Breakfast Ashore

There was nothing we could do so we made the best of a bad job and left. We had been told to report back to the ship by noon so we made enquiries from people we met outside on how to get to the dockyard and caught the bus When we arrived it seemed that the whole ship's company were standing on the dockside. I made my way over to the Coxswain and, while we were waiting for some of the officers to arrive we exchanged experiences. He had been taken to a house quite near the dockyard, the home of a dockyard workman. They could not do enough for him and, despite the rationing had served him with a stew he said was marvellous for his dinner and for breakfast piles and piles on what looked like pancakes with sugar and lemon

I told him of our experience and when I came to the part about rations he told me that he had onboard ration cards that had to be issued to all men staying ashore. Due to the situation prevailing he had not been able to issue them. We learned from the rest of the ship's company that the lack of ration cards had not affected their reception. By far the majority spoke very highly of the warm welcome the people of Glasgow had given them.

The officers arrived and the Captain addressed the ship's company. Repairs were anticipated to take nine days. One half of the ship's company would go on four days leave followed by the other half. There was an enormous cheer and everyone, on being dismissed, rushed onboard to get the things they would need either to go on leave or stay ashore for the next four days. The Coxswain asked me to give him a hand making out travel warrants and ration cards as we wanted to get those going on leave away as soon as possible. In addition we had to issue ration cards to those billeted ashore. We found it more practical to line the men up and make out their forms as they supplied the details rather than going through the ship's ledger. Each ration card had to have their name written on it and be stamped and signed. Each rail warrant was the same except we had to fill in the destination.

We rapidly dropped into a routine in which I filled in their names and the Coxswain did the rest. Even so it took over two hours before the last man going on leave left the ship and then we had to start on the ration cards for the others. The ships galley was out of action and there was no way of supplying a midday meal to the rest of the men. We approached the Captain for a possible solution but he was as baffled as we were and expressed the opinion that we should get their ration cards to them as soon as possible and send them back to their billets. The Coxswain then had an idea and made about three telephone calls. I was busy making out the ration cards to concern myself with what he was doing.

He came back in the ship's office with a big grin but wouldn't tell me what it was all about. We carried on working for about a quarter of an hour when we heard horns blowing and a big commotion outside.

We immediately went to investigate and there, pulled up alongside the ship, were four mobile food canteens. They were manned by the W.V.S. (women's voluntary service) and would normally be on railway stations and at service men's recreational facilities. They had opened them up and were already serving hot tea and sandwiches made of those famous scotch rolls and hot sausage meat. The Coxswain had called and found the headquarters of the W.V.S. When he called and told his story they asked him how many men and then said to wait and they would be along soon.

They were as good as their word and they had diverted their full complement of canteens to the dockyard. We couldn't thank them enough and this was the real face of Glasgow.

Everyone had at least one sandwich and hot tea and we resumed our task of issuing the ration cards to the men in billets. I learned it was impossible except by going back to the same billeting officer to get my billet changed and I knew what his answer would be. I filled out four ration cards for the signalman and myself. We were only supposed to have two, one each, but I felt, under the circumstances we were going to need them.

The routine was that the cards had to be handed over to the people at the house where you were billeted or you could purchase the rationed goods yourself and take them in. We were given a ten-shilling advance for expenses and the billeting people had to submit their bills through the appropriate channels for whatever they provided in accommodation and food. I decided we would buy our own rations and it was the best decision I made for some time.

We took the bus back to our billets. I had seen in the morning, a group of small shops near where we had caught the bus. The butchers shop was empty and by the look of the marble slabs on which his good were normally laid out he was out of stock. He greeted us with enthusiasm, shook our hands and asked what he could do for us. I showed him one of the ration cards and explained we each had one. He asked where we were staying and by his frown and response I guessed he was familiar with our landlady.

The ration cards were a mystery to me. I did not know what we were entitled to buy, what was on ration and what was not. He soon enlightened me and the amount seemed frightfully small. Two ounces of bacon each, two ounces of meat each, one egg, etc., etc. He went to the big cold cupboard at the back of the shop and lifted out a side of bacon from which he sliced four thin rashers, this was our bacon for the week. He then suggested for our meat ration we take a pork chop each, which we did. I looked at the little pile despairingly. How could we live for four days on that? He saw my face and smiled, don't worry he said and went back to the cold cupboard.

He pulled out a tray full of what looked like meatballs as big as tennis balls. These are called "Savoury Duck" he said, "They are not rationed because they are made from unrationed liver etc." I never found out what the etc. was but I do know they were delicious when cooked. He gave us four of these then he added a small roll of black pudding for each of us, a piece of Liver and some tripe. I hadn't seen tripe since I was a youngster and the signalman looked at it with a very hesitant look. I thought of the lovely tripe and onions my mother used to make during the depression and determined I was going to cook it myself.

During this dispensing of such largesse he kept up a constant conversation about the war and the news of the Bismarck and how he was certain we were winning. After wrapping the food up and putting it in a brown carrier bag he made one request "If anyone asks where you got this lot tell them the navy issued it or something like that but please do not mention my shop". He had done nothing illegal but in those days of shortages his customers, particularly the one we were billeted on would probably complain.

He then told us to follow him and led us into the bakery next door. He joked with the lady behind the counter, obviously a daily occurrence and then told her who we were and where we were staying. The woman was not as inhibited as him and said "I didn't think that Lady Muck would allow common sailors in her house," she obviously knew our landlady quite well and didn't mind who knew how she felt. In addition to bakery she sold eggs and a variety of pies made from goodness knows what. She started off by giving us two eggs each despite the ration of one. She then put a loaf of fresh bread on the counter. It was actually two loaves joined together but apparently this is how it was sold. She then put several of the small pies with the bread and then apologised that she only had a few rolls left over and gave us about six of them. She added some sweet cakes and then started to put them all in a big brown paper bag.

As a last item she put a small packet of margarine and a small packet of butter into the bag. The butcher still had our two ration cards in his hand and between them they took off the appropriate coupons. I had not paid the butcher so offered him the ten shilling note. He said "Nonsense, nonsense Lad." Giving me the ration cards he waved goodbye and marched out of the shop. I offered the money to the lady and she also refused payment. All I could do was to thank her and we left to walk over to greengrocer. Here we encountered a man and his wife who seemed to be having a constant argument.

I found it impossible to understand what they were saying to each other as for a few moments we stood in the shop and they were ignorant of our presence. They turned and saw us and the woman came over with a big smile, "Don't pay any attention to him," she said, nodding towards her grinning husband, "he would rather argue about football than eat, now what can I do for you?" I explained our circumstances and where we were staying adding that I felt it was better to take our own food in rather than bother the landlady. "How are you going to cook it?" she asked. I said that either the landlady would cook it or I would. At this, she and her husband really laughed. He said, "I would love to see her face when you tell her that."

The woman asked me how things were in the billet. I didn't want to get into any explanation so I just said it wasn't very pleasant but we would only be there for four or five days. She said that they lived above the shop and only had the one bedroom or she would be delighted to put us up. I then started to select the few things like potatoes etc. that we would need. She had a discussion with her husband then came back and said, "Do you have ration cards?" I explained that I did not think I needed them for potatoes etc. "You don't, but I have a proposal for you," I told her we had ration cards but I had already used up the weeks supply in the bags were carrying.

“My proposal is that you come over here for every meal including breakfast,” I was astounded, she had only just met us and was offering so much. I turned to the young signalman but I could see he was already in favour of the idea. I showed her what we had in the bags and she was delighted. We went up to her flat for a cup of tea and it was arranged that we would come to their place at 8.30, 1 o’clock and 6 o’clock for our meals. I gave her the extra two ration cards and we left for our billet.

When we arrived back the landlady greeted us almost at the door with a demand for our ration cards. I told her that we were going to buy our own rations and she could have them cooked. She point blank refused when I added that I would make out a list of what we wanted for our different meals. The signalman had to turn away to keep from laughing; he knew I was really turning the screw.

I then told her that if that were her attitude we would eat all our meals out and only use the house for accommodation. She turned away but with a parting shot, “You’ll be lucky,” she said. She didn’t know we had already been lucky and for the next four days we would vanish at breakfast time and not come back until after supper. She was curious and furious but she never found out how we were getting fed.

The ship was in a terrible mess with dockyard workmen climbing all over the place. Naturally when compelled to stay in for one type of repair all outstanding items are tackled and modifications made. In this way they added depth charge throwers. These looked like an empty oil drum on a mounting and sloped out from the ship. The idea was, and it worked very well, that the depth charges would be literally thrown clear of the ship and cover a much wider area than the stern dropped charges. We used them and found them very efficient. Our turn for leave arrived and we left the billet without a single expression of farewell or regret on either side. It had been a bad experience but a very isolated one. I found that by far the greatest majority of the ship’s company had been treated extremely well and many had made lasting friendships. The four days leave simply flew by particularly when we had to spend a third of it in the train getting there and back. However, like all leave it was well worth it and I arrived back somewhat refreshed.

We left Clydebank and returned to our base at Rosyth to take up our east coast convoy escort duties again. The total change had been a boost for all of us although during our stay we had to draft out several of our experienced company and take on brand new entries. This time was always an anxious time for all of us.

The problem was that the new men would inevitably have to be trained to do their job and when this job was as vital as manning the guns, the depth charges, the close range weapons etc the others with them had to be twice as fast until they were competent. Add to this the sea sickness, the whole horrible change over from a life ashore, no matter how hard, to a life that was infinitely harder and it becomes clear how anxious a ship's company can be until they can rely on them.

One thing that never ceased to amaze me was the courage, the fortitude and the cheerful acceptance of the hardships that the new men and new officers had. They were in a world that, to them, must at first have been absolute hell yet they performed magnificently. I used to wonder if I could have displayed such characteristics if I had been thrown into it like they had. The majority had only a few weeks training and, in fact, did not know one end of a ship from another. As for the naval terms we used as a matter of course we had to explain them until they understood what was wanted.

Our arrival back alongside in Rosyth went practically unnoticed and within a few hours we were back in the full routine of topping up with everything from tinned pilchards to fuel oil. The Captain and the officer doing supply duties went ashore and I collected all the accumulated signals, A.F.O's (Admiralty Fleet Orders) and miscellaneous correspondence relating to the Confidential books. I hated this bit because in the A.F.O. and other correspondence there was always a long list of corrections to the signal books and the other manuals.

I settled down at my desk in the wheelhouse and proceeded to insert and delete for the next few hours. It was a time consuming and dreary job but essential as the corrections and amendments were in effect the moment they were received. It would have been a disaster to misinterpret a signal or not be able to decypher one due to the non-entry of an amendment. It has happened but fortunately not to me. I did however have one incident that created a major problem due to this correction system.

When this incident happened we were in convoy, as usual, and we ran into thick fog just south of Folkestone where the channel was very narrow and the sand shoals visible on either side at low tide. We were heading north. This is a dangerous situation on your own but with twenty or more ships it is hazardous in the extreme. The only thing to do is to maintain rigidly the course and speed and sound the siren at appropriate intervals. I became aware that someone was using their siren to send sound signals by Morse.

I could make out the Morse but the two-letter signal did not make any sense. Being night-time did not help any and I tried reading the meaning in the convoy signal book by the means of the red light we had to use to preserve our night vision. The two-letter signal was for the use of a convoy Commodore and meant reverse course. I reported this to the Captain and he couldn't believe it. A thought struck me as I had a vague memory of making a couple of amendments to the book. I picked up a small box lamp that had a very tiny aperture and shone it on the page. The red ink that had deleted the signal was immediately visible making the signal obsolete. I showed this to the Captain and he really did get upset. We maintained our course but wondered how many of the convoy would obey this mistaken and very dangerous manoeuvre.

We were completely helpless. We couldn't cancel the signal, we couldn't get in touch with the Commodore; we could do nothing but wait. When dawn came we had about twelve ships with us maintaining their course so somewhere we had mislaid at least three ships including the Commodore. We signalled our rear escort and told him to move up, we were going back to see what had happened. We put on speed and two hours later we sighted ships on the northern course and closed them. The Commodore was the leading ship and over the loud hailer the Captain asked what had happened.

The Commodore replied that he had considered the situation too hazardous and had therefore decided to reverse the convoy course and proceed back to harbour. However he realised that the channel was too narrow and had made a sound signal cancelling his order and resumed his original course. Unfortunately, like ourselves, many of the ships had not heard the cancellation and some of them had reversed course. I could see that it was taking the Captain all his time not to blast out but he restrained himself and told the Commodore we would go back to find the missing ships. A little time later we spotted the missing two ships, one was standing by another that had run aground on a shoal. The tide was coming in and it would be high water in about an hour. Unfortunately we were in an area that if reconnaissance spotted us the grounded vessel would be a sitting duck.

It was decided to try and pull her off by attaching a cable to her forward winch and to our stern bollards. A line was shot across, which they pulled in, followed by a rope attached to a steel cable. The whole exercise was carried out very quickly and once secured the Captain ordered engines to go slow ahead. There were a few moments of anxiety as the steel cable stretched and started that singing noise that precedes a break but suddenly the cable went slack as the ship moved. We towed her clear and the Master signalled his thanks and said he would rejoin the convoy. We left him and put on speed to join the Commodore and it took us two days to finally put the convoy together again.

Following this incident, on arrival back in harbour a letter was sent to the C in C recommending that all future corrections should be done in black ink and a black star should be place alongside all previously corrected signals. To my chagrin we received a letter that stated that all corrections had always been made in black ink and the use of red ink was a personal and unfortunate choice. Naturally, the Captain felt I had let him down when he received the letter and sent for me to tell me so.

After telling me the contents of the letter he asked for an explanation. I told him whoever had advised the Admiral, probably his flag lieutenant, either didn't know what he was talking about or was trying to cover up the fact that he had not been following the Admiralty laid down procedure with his books. I went and dug out the Admiralty Fleet Order dated many years back and renewed annually that spelled out the technique for correcting signal books. It made specific reference to the use of red ink in order to avoid any confusion between the old entry and the new.

The Captain replied in a letter to the Admiral quoting the A.F.O. and adding a further suggestion that the Admiral might be pleased to inform Admiralty of the hazard that had been revealed. We received a very nice letter in which we were told that appropriate action had been taken both locally and with Admiralty. I would have like to have heard the appropriate action between the Admiral and his Flag Lieutenant.

In the change over that had taken place I had to let two experienced signalman go and with only a total staff of one Leading Signalman and four signalmen it was a severe blow. However the two newcomers on first glance seemed acceptable. One had three badges that indicated a minimum service of twelve years so I congratulated myself on having him. The other was a man in his thirties whose total exposure to the navy and to signals was about six weeks. He turned out to be an extremely nice person and a willing learner. I was in for an awful shock. Going down the Forth was usually a very quiet time and after casting off and getting into mid stream I usually went to the wheelhouse safe and brought the books up to the bridge where I could get at them easily. I left the three-badge signalman on the bridge to take care of anything that came along.

I was sorting out the books when an urgent call came for me. I rushed up to the bridge completely baffled at what could possibly cause a panic. I looked around and ahead of us was a destroyer also on his way out. At his yardarm he had hoisted a group of flags which when decoded gave us his speed. This was a matter of courtesy. I looked at our yardarm and our answering pendant was dipped indicating we had seen the flags but did not yet know their meaning.

I ordered it close up as the signal was so common it was self evident, I reported it's meaning, the other ship must have been a bit puzzled at the long time but everything was hauled down. The Captain adjusted our speed so we would not overtake and I went over and asked the signalman what the problem was. He replied that he did not know what the flags were. I couldn't believe my ears; it seemed impossible.

His explanation was perfectly simple and logical to him. He had joined the Royal Navy in the last few months of World War 1. He had, at that time been trained as a signalman. When the war ended he was discharged and joined the reserves. Apparently, in the reserve navy there were two types of entry. One was the type that required attendance at drills every week. The other was simply being on the books in case of emergency. A payment was made in both cases but the second case was a very small amount. He had opted for the second case and except for receiving the money and letters at the appropriate time telling him he had been awarded a good conduct badge he did nothing but be available. He had been driving a brewers dray (a horse drawn wagon that delivered beer) for about twenty years.

This made our lives terribly difficult. The newcomer could not be left alone until he had experience. This man could never possibly assimilate the fundamentals necessary to ever act as a signalman. At least the other man had learnt the Morse code and the colours of the flags. The powers that be however hadn't given even the most rudimentary instructions to the older man, assuming he was, as it said in his papers, a qualified signalman. From then on we went into three watches and, in addition to my constant commitment I had to stand a permanent morning watch with the younger newcomer. I must say however that the cause of all this felt terrible about it and, during the day was always there to get anything we needed and during the night he would arrive at all hours with cocoa etc.

The guns crews were also suffering from this dilution of skill and constant exercise on the guns were the order of the day until they could get ammunition from the ready use lockers and the magazine and load the gun with their eyes closed. The test under action conditions had to come and it was a feeling of tension we waited the first attack.

We joined the convoy at Methil and it was larger than usual, thirty ships. The destroyer that had gone ahead of us was the rear escort and he was well experienced on this run. With the usual mixing and milling around we got under way and soon we were past May Island on our way south. I realise that to the reader, if I described every convoy (which I have no intention of doing) it would, despite the action, become repetitive and possibly boring. I can however describe certain incidents, which became memorable to me and gave a picture of the whole situation.

We moved south and the weather became rough. There was a strong wind springing up from the South-West and within an hour we were taking it green over the forecastle. She dug her bows into it until the whole of the forecastle vanished below the water and it seemed from the bridge as if we were on an island. She shuddered slightly from side to side then like a huge whale her bows came up clear of the water. The roar of the receding wave was deafening.

The forward gun was of course manned and the gun's crew was huddled behind the gunshield trying in vain to keep dry. The waves in their rush aft would hit the superstructure under the bridge where the ready use locker of ammunition was stored and bounce back drenching the gun's crew. None of this was, of course, unusual; it was a frequent occurrence. The difference was that half of the Gun's crew were brand new and already were so sick they could barely stand. It was at this crucial moment the lookout spotted the bombers. They were the high level kind; they would be within the range of our guns before they started their bombing run.

Action stations were sounded and we moved clear of the convoy to give a clear line of vision to the director. The order open fire when ready was passed and the sound of the double bell that precedes every shot was heard and then we were in the thick of the battle. I had time to look at the forward gun, which was now pointing to starboard and skywards so I could see every move. I will never forget that sight. Men who had been paralysed with seasickness were grabbing shells from the ready use lockers and literally fighting their way to the gun. Because they were totally unused to the movement of the ship they could not anticipate the roll and the lift. As a result a wave would sweep down and catch them with a shell clutched in their arms.

It swept them back and bashed them against the lockers and they lay in the scuppers trying desperately to regain their foothold. The Petty Officer who was Captain of the gun divided his time between helping them to their feet, getting shells, loading the gun and trying to keep up morale. One man, a lawyer in peace time, clutched a shell with his arms wrapped round it and was repeatedly bashed back against the superstructure but he refused to give in and forced his way to the gun.

Despite this the gun kept up a constant barrage although far slower between rounds than it had ever been. The bombers released their bombs but there were no casualties. The men had bruises all over but fortunately no broken bones. It was a terrible introduction to the kind of life they could expect but they took it to a large extent in their stride.

One of the worst incidents occurred when it seemed a combination of circumstances had conspired against us. The enemy had been laying mines and this time he had laid mines in the shallow channel on the south east coast. The minesweepers had been out and to all intents and purposes had cleared the channel. It was just after sunset when we reached the area where we could expect E boat attack and sure enough they appeared. The night was intensely black with no moon and overcast with clouds.

How they did it I will never know but suddenly they were among the convoy. It was impossible to fire on them without hitting the merchant ships. The first dull explosion of a torpedo was felt through the ship, certainly one ship had been hit, then in horrible rapid sequence came two more. We were racing around the convoy trying to get a sight of the enemy. The lookout caught sight of them. There were two of them steering a course away from the convoy at high speed. We opened fire with every thing we had and had the satisfaction of seeing one of them dissolve into flames.

At that moment we heard and felt another explosion, the enemy was still with us. We turned and ploughed our way through the convoy, as it was obvious the E boats were between the coast and the ships. As we approached the convoy we heard the shouting of men in the water and they were cheering and calling thinking we were going to pick them up. I could vaguely make some of them out by the little lights the odd one carried on his life jacket. Their voices grew louder as we approached, then to their dismay and our absolute horror we had to go through them as an E boat was speeding up the convoy beyond them. We opened fire with the short-range weapons and she stopped her attack, turned away and left at high speed.

The tug designated as rescue ship closed in and started to pick up survivors. We had lost two ships with a third damaged but not in danger of sinking. She was ordered into the nearest port. It is a strange feeling and one that must be guarded against but after an intense action you feel that it is over now and you can relax and start to repair the damage. This is a very dangerous feeling and had to be pushed on one side as the enemy could immediately come in for a further attack. In this case they didn't and we rounded up the ships and plodded along as usual.

However on this trip they hadn't finished with us yet. We were at dawn action stations and the day was bright and clear as the sun came up. Without warning a ship in the middle of the column exploded. She had hit a mine but it was a complete puzzle as several ships had passed over the water without incident.

We went over, dropped scrambling nets and pulled survivors out of the water. There were not many and two of them died as they were laid out on the deck smothered in oil fuel. The ship's company did everything they could to clean off the survivors and we rejoined the convoy. It was then I read a light signal from one of the ships in the convoy. "Ship ahead of me is laying mines." It was unbelievable but it would account for the mystery of the sinking.

The Captain closed the ship while I was sending a signal to the Commodore. He ordered the ship out of the column to seaward, which she did. We circled her with all guns trained on her and with the loud hailer told her to head into harbour. He ordered our rear escort to accompany her until our own MTB's could come out and take over. The ship was flying the Norwegian flag and had joined the convoy in London. Her registration was correct in every way but she had been taken over by the enemy, rigged with mine laying equipment and had already sailed in two convoys.

The stern door through which she had dropped the mines only opened just enough, swinging up from the bottom to let a mine through. It required intense observation at a very specific time to see what she was doing. Fortunately the master of the ship that had been astern of the ship that was sunk was suspicious and had an observer posted with orders not to miss a thing. They had seen her drop a mine and had taken violent avoiding action and it went harmlessly by missing all the ships.

The German invasion of Norway had taken place and suddenly we were ordered to proceed with utmost despatch to rendezvous with several other ships at a point off the Norwegian coast. The weather was very good and we made good time, reporting to the senior officer present for our orders. They were very simple, escort the escaping Norwegian ships to the nearest of our ports.

We didn't have to ask what ships, as far as the eye could see there were ships of every shape and size. Some of them were seagoing yachts but the majority were small sailing boats, some were just fifteen foot or twenty foot boats designed for weekend fishing in calm waters powered by small outboard engines. We circled them and prayed for good weather. Should a storm hit, which was not uncommon in those waters, at least half of them would never survive.

For some reason, on that day, the expected aircraft attack never came. Except for a submarine scare that turned out to be one of our own the first day was uneventful. In the morning, which dawned bright and clear, the ships, boats and other craft were still plodding along. A couple of the yachts had taken a small boat in tow. In other cases petrol had been passed over to some of the boats using outboard engines.

The first attack came out of the rising sun and consisted of four fighter-bombers low over the water. Our lookouts spotted them, our guns were already loaded and they opened fire within seconds of the warning.

It was barrage firing and the aircraft entered the black clouds of the exploding shells before they knew what was happening. Their formation broke and they went in all directions. We knew they would either form up again or try individual attacks so everyone scanned the skies with a great deal of intensity. The sky was full of high-scattered clouds in which, or above which, they could take shelter.

Suddenly the starboard point five opened up with all four barrels and his tracer were parallel to the sea. We had all been concentrating on the sky but one aircraft was coming in at sea level practically wave hopping. The Lewis and the Oerlikon joined the fray pouring a solid sheet of lead and exploding shells in the aircraft's direction.

As the aircraft came closer it seemed to bear a charmed life as it's machine guns opened up and the spurts they created came straight for the ship. At this point it was both normal and prudent to put a sheet of metal between you and the oncoming bullets, which we did by ducking below the bridge superstructure. The men manning the close range weapons were supposed to do this for the few seconds the aircraft run would take.

The point five machine gun did not stop as expected and kept up a hail of fire until the aircraft was over us and therefore out of his firing line. As it passed over a trail of smoke and fire could be seen coming from the aircraft. It kept going low over the water and we watched it until it vanished with spurts of flame and smoke issuing from it. The other aircraft seemed to have vanished and we resumed our plodding with the "Odds and Sods" flotilla as the men called them. That day there were no more alarms and the next day we were under a large fighter cover as we approached the mine barrier laid by the Navy all down the East Coast. We were ordered to leave and return to Rosyth to pick up where we left off.

CHAPTER FIFTEEN

'Wiggy'

The incident with the point five machine guns can only be explained by talking about the man who manned that particular gun. His name was "Wiggy" Birkett; why they nicknamed him Wiggy I will never know. He was born and raised in the slums of Liverpool and had joined the Royal Navy Reserve at the age of fifteen before the war. The ship to which he reported for reserve training once a week was the Wallace and when war was declared he, and many others like him commissioned the Wallace and saw her through her conversion.

He belonged to a close community formed by the Liverpudlians, or "Scouses", as they were known by the others onboard. The common nickname for people from Liverpool was "Scouse" and their very distinctive dialect made it quite clear where they were born and raised. If Wiggy had attended school at any time he hid the fact as if he was ashamed of it. He spoke to me one day a few days after I joined the ship. He was doing temporary duty as the Bosun's mate at the back of the bridge. His duty was to be available to be sent on messages or to be sent round the ship piping orders.

He produced a letter, it was very badly written and misspelled, and he asked me to read it to him. All this was done in secrecy behind the Directing position, which hid us from view. To this day I am pleased that something told me to accept this request as if it happened every day. He was watching my face closely and I knew that the slightest wrong gesture on my part would turn him away. I read the letter to him quietly, correcting it in part to make it more understandable as whoever had written it had used some words I simply could not decipher but the context told me what they should be.

He stood there quietly but he was beaming with pleasure. The letter was from a girl he had met on his last leave and I must say, although her writing and spelling left much to be desired, she gave the impression of a very pleasant girl who had been duly impressed with Wiggy and wanted to correspond with him.

As I finished the letter with the request for a reply in the last sentence I saw the smile leave his face. He reached out for the letter and thanked me and then went to turn away. I stopped him and asked him if he could write a reply. He looked shamefaced and said

"No, I can't write." I said, "That is no problem, there are lots of people who can't write." His face brightened and I was pleased with my white lie. "When you want to reply come and see me and we'll do it together," I said.

This was the beginning of a long involvement in Wiggy's love affair that went on until I left the ship. Some times it was hilarious as he told me what he wanted to say and I converted it into none dialect English. The one I remember most vividly was his first letter in reply. He covered all the subjects she had spoken about in her letter and there was no problem getting it down legibly. He may not have been able to read or write but his mind was as clear and sharp as a tack. But on this sentence he had me beaten. He started it by asking how to spell slongers. I did not understand but I was being very cautious in order not to offend him. I asked him what was the sentence he wanted me to write. He said it was "Slongers your all right I'm all right". I explained that it was written as three words, "So long as." He thought that was great and ever after he would sign off using the same words carefully enunciated as three words.

Needless to say there were several among the "Scouses" in the same predicament as Wiggy so, in harbour, not long after the mail came onboard I would take up station near the funnel or in the deserted wheelhouse if it was raining and of course Wiggy would be the first to arrive and when he left there would be one or two others. These men were the salt of the earth and proved it time and time again in conditions that would have made even the most courageous of men cringe.

When Wiggy was questioned about his continuing to fire despite the machine gun firing sweeping towards him he replied he that could see the twin pattern as the shells hit the water and knew they would hit either side of him. I must admit I shuddered when I heard him tell the First Lieutenant his reason. Although he was correct and the shells had ricocheted off the forecastle forward and gone through the funnel aft leaving the bridge unscathed the risk he took was enormous. What can anyone say to a man like that? The First Lieutenant told him that he must never again make such a judgement but must follow the orders laid down. Wiggy accepted this with a shrug but in a burst of confidence one day he said it didn't make much sense.

I am afraid that Wiggy's absolute familiarity with the point- five machine gun led him into somewhat careless behaviour. One day we were taking on oil from an oiler lying alongside. Wiggy was cleaning the gun and did not check that the previous watch had cleared the gun properly as there was always a round left in each barrel after the belts were removed. These had to be removed manually. He pointed the gun over the head of the oiler and eased the spring. To his horror four shells fired and passed through the bridge and funnel of the oiler. Fortunately no one was hurt but the Captain of the oiler took a great deal of placating in order that he did not make a case out of the incident.

Another time he removed the stops that prevented the gun from being swung too far forward or astern and thus hitting the ship. He had done this as part of a legitimate cleaning procedure for greasing the channels that the gun rode on. Apparently "Stand Easy" had been piped, (this is the ten minute break during the forenoon) and he left and when he came back he forgot. The next time we went into action he followed an E Boat racing down the side. The gun should have stopped training but it didn't so he perforated the Whaler that was on the davits in a dozen places rendering it useless. Wiggy was in trouble again and was punished by having his leave stopped for a month. As we did not get ashore very much it was no hardship.

We sailed after this incident and the Captain noticed a new face on the point five's. "Where is Birkett?" he wanted to know. A young sub who had been designated the divisional officer for Wiggy's part of ship, told the Captain he had taken him off that duty altogether and given him the Bosun's mate duties. They walked to one side of the bridge and discussed it quietly. A short time later I saw Wiggy entering the sponson and relieving the other man. I must admit I breathed a sigh of relief when I saw this happen. You can't beat experience backed by courage.

I learned a tremendous amount from Wiggy and his friends. The most important thing I learned, and it has carried me a long way, was never believe that intelligence and education go hand in hand. When I became the President of a civilian company after I left the Navy this fact was brought home to me with redoubled force. No matter how many degrees the employee or potential employee had, they could not be taken as proof of his or her ability.

I found people with PhDs who, when faced with decisions or action to be taken outside their specialisation bumbled blindly along where Wiggy and his friends would have taken the situation in their stride. The problem is of course the type of employee, who, because he or she has a degree, refuses to accept advice from those they consider to be lesser mortals. Naturally this is not an all-embracing statement as I have met far more to whom the opposite applies but one has to be careful not to judge by paper qualifications

CHAPTER SIXTEEN

Matelots

Talking about Wiggy reminded me that I had not really touched on the men with whom I spent three years of the most critical time in my life. In the confined space we lived, ate, slept and had our being there was no room for antagonism. There had to be an acceptance of everyone's idiosyncrasies (and believe me there were many) an acceptance of their religion, politics even their table manners.

We had to be closer than brothers because in the overall scheme of things, brothers can quarrel and make up. Men thrown together as we were did not have the luxury of quarrelling to let off steam as a hasty word could create a schism that would not heal and life would be unpleasant. It is impossible to describe them all in detail but I have tried a few thumbnail sketches.

The senior man in the mess was the Coxswain; in fact he was the senior man on the lower deck. His action station was at the wheel and in the middle of action, when all hell seemed to be breaking loose, his methodical and measured reply to course changes emanating from the voice pipe in a calm voice had a steadying influence on all the bridge personnel.

Cock Clout, an old time petty officer whose duty was Chief Boatswains Mate who had not hesitated to plunge into a blazing inferno of a compartment to rescue a dockyard worker whose welding torch had ignited a drum of highly inflammable paint. The man survived and Clout had only superficial burns, however he lost the uniform he was in together with everything in his pockets and a prized wrist watch. The Navy approved the cost of a replacement uniform after much haggling but would not replace any of his personal possessions. When the dockyard workers heard of this, while we were at sea, they had a collection and on arrival presented him with a lovely watch and wallet and other items that he had listed as lost to the Navy to support his claim. As a messmate he was great and in action he displayed the same disregard of his own safety in supporting his guns crew.

The Petty Officer Telegraphist Pony Moore, a very close friend of mine whose practical jokes showed a devious mind that kept us in fits of laughter at whoever was his latest victim. Coming alongside after a long and arduous trip, while coming up the Forth he had rigged the shower so at a touch of a tap he could freeze the poor unfortunate under the shower. He was stripped naked in the bathroom alongside the Chief Stoker who was under the shower when he pulled his new dodge.

The Chief immediately went for him and he, roaring with laughter and stark naked ran out on the upper deck. Unfortunately we were just pulling alongside and the welcome home party headed by the Admiral, several senior officers and their wives had a first class view of a naked sailor running on the upper deck. It did cause a bit of an uproar but nothing came of it and it blew over except for the story, much embellished which went round the local ships. On one occasion when we were in danger of sinking he sent his staff out and stayed at the key until he was knee deep in oil and water. We didn't sink but he constantly complained about losing a good pair of trousers.

The Chief Stoker, who imagined himself to be a strict disciplinarian with the stokers and engine room staff, was a great source of gentle amusement to them. He would huff and puff and raise his voice and swear at an offending stoker, the next minute he would be making sure, during action, that they were well looked after. He was the one who rigged himself a bunk in the generator room, which was perforated by E boat cannon shell. He never lived it down as they all said that Hitler had smelled his pipe (which he smoked constantly) and ordered him to be removed for pollution.

Then there was the Supply Petty Officer who, although pushing 35 was unmarried and considered himself the Navy's gift to the female population of every port we visited. He was engaged to three women in different ports at the same time and had a heck of a time juggling his correspondence. His philandering was brought to an abrupt end when, on entering Rosyth, there were messages from two of them that they had checked into a certain hotel and would be waiting for him when he arrived back.

Neither of them was aware of the other and here they were in the same hotel. It took great persuasion and several tots to get his friend, the Gunners mate, to deliver a note personally to each of them at the hotel telling them that due to an emergency with his mother, he had left the ship and gone home. In action, he manned the sick bay with the sick berth attendant and the Doctor, when we had one. His care and compassion was a legend with any survivors we picked up and with our own odd casualty.

The Gunner's Mate, a petty officer, was a very small man with a very loud voice. His stentorian bellow could be heard all over the ship during gun exercise drill. At first he terrified the new entries when they came onboard but the others told them not to worry he was "All gate and gaiters". The gaiters referred to the fact that in the gunnery school where these gunners' mates were trained, they had to wear gaiters round the bottom of their trousers. Don't ask me why.

In action he was sometimes in the Director from which all guns are trained and fired but more commonly he was on the forward or after gun urging the men to greater efforts. I have seen him in the middle of intense action take over from a new seaman as a loading number and while ramming shells home keeping up a running commentary of gun drill. Never once did he give a new man a bad time during or after his first action. They made tremendous efforts to please him.

With so many men I can but touch on these few but in courage and comradeship every member of the ship's company deserved a paragraph. On the darkest night when it was impossible to make out the face of the person next to you I learned to recognise every man who ever came on the bridge by his voice. The variety of dialects helped and for many years when I heard someone speak with a dialect I could place him within a few miles of where he lived. At the same time recalling the face and name of the shipmate long gone in an instant flash of nostalgia.

To give the impression that the ship's company were a group of well behaved, god fearing and law abiding citizens would be ludicrous. They did all the things to let off steam that every normal sailor did. They were bailed out of jail occasionally so the ship did not have to sail short-handed. They sang rude songs walking down the main street when returning onboard. They drank too much but they looked after the ones who became too drunk. They went to local dance halls and, to the chagrin of the local boys, constantly excused their partners so they could dance. These and a dozen other things they did to plague the local population. At least they were very popular with the ladies.

Of course in mentioning ladies thoughts inevitably turn to sex. However, they were no different than any other men whether civilian soldier or airmen. Their reputation had come down to them through the ages; a totally undeserved reputation but one that time and tide will never dispel. They were as faithful to their wives and sweethearts as the wives and sweethearts were to them. Until they made some kind of an attachment or commitment they were no better and certainly no worse than anyone else.

The problem for sailors is that they have little time for the courting process. As a result one night in port had to be crammed with the experiences that other men living a more stable existence could take days or even weeks to achieve. The navy, in the training ships gave long and miserable lectures accompanied by graphic slides on the dangers of sex. I must admit that at 15 it frightened me to death. They made it so bad that I took ages to believe that females were really nice people.

The "One night stand" as it was popularly referred to was the fact of life to most sailors. As the saying goes, "It takes two to Tango" so there was no shortage of young ladies who were most willing to Tango with someone they thought they would never see again. Most sailors did not want or need to go with professionals; there were quite enough females eager and willing to have a good time. I remember one instance, though, that should be recorded for posterity.

Onboard we had a tall good-looking sailor called Jenkins. He was well over six feet tall and was referred to as, of course, Lofty Jenkins. We were in Rosyth and the ship gave overnight leave. Lofty went to Edinburgh to scout out the potential entertainment for the evening. In a pub down Leith Walk, he was picked up by (as he described it) a lovely luscious lady. They had a wonderful evening together, the pub followed by a dance hall followed by sausage sandwiches and tea at a mobile canteen.

He escorted the young lady to what he thought were her lodgings. These turned out to be a very old fashioned house that had been turned into a bed and breakfast place. She invited him in and of course he most willingly went. In the large bedroom she broke the news that she only worked for money. By this time Lofty had made up his mind how the evening out would end and although disappointed he produced the money she asked for. She then proceeded to undress and place her clothes in the cupboard. Lofty just threw his on the chairs. He turned in as she went down the hall to the bathroom. He lay in bed for over half an hour until he finally got impatient. He knew she had to return as her clothes were in the cupboard so he though she was chatting it up with a girl friend or something.

After an hour passed he could no longer curb his impatience and he went to the cupboard where she had hung her clothes. When he opened it there was no clothes. It was a dumb waiter and she had absconded and pulled her clothes down, dressed and left the place. Lofty was furious, he questioned the night man in the lobby but could get nothing out of him. He went back to the room, slept, had breakfast in the morning and when they presented him with the bill he told them to give it to the young lady. When they kicked up a fuss he suggested they call the police and that finished the situation.

We thought that was the end of the story. As our base was Rosyth overnight leave to Edinburgh was possible on rare occasions. When we arrived in and when it was possible, Lofty would bribe someone with his tot of rum to change watches with him so he could get ashore. We found out later that he spent hours walking down Leith Walk or on Princess Street always hoping to find the young lady. It was at least six months or more later when he came onboard grinning like a Cheshire cat. She had picked him up in the same pub and to her he was just another sailor. To his absolute astonishment she had completely forgotten him. She went through her pick up performance but this time it was late at night and they headed straight back to her lodgings.

The routine was played out in exactly the same place and in exactly the same way. However, when she left to supposedly go to the bathroom, Lofty jumped out of bed, grabbed her clothes from the dumb waiter then watched with satisfaction as it descended empty. He pushed her clothes under the bed and sure enough, in a few minutes she arrived dressed only in the slip she had left in. She demanded to know what he had done with her clothes. He played innocent for a while asking her why she needed her clothes. Finally she lost her temper and screamed at him and when that didn't work she offered him his money back.

He was totally unmoved and then he announced his intention to take her to the police and also the proprietor without whose connivance she could not work her racket. She could see he was absolutely serious because he told her how he had looked for her for months. She then started to plead with him and he told her he would be satisfied if he got what he originally came for. At this point in telling the story he would grin and say that they had reached a very satisfactory agreement as far as he was concerned but in the morning she had insisted that she was not that kind of a girl.

CHAPTER SEVENTEEN

Hospitalisation

There were many times I was grateful for the group of men that comprised the Chief and Petty Officers mess but never more so than when I was hospitalised. We were in convoy and on this occasion instead of going into the Forth we had to go further north to escort a special couple of ships to a rendezvous where they would be taken over by another escort. As luck would have it I had been feeling quite ill during the day but hadn't complained as I thought we would be going alongside that night where we would have access to the Doctor.

The message came that prevented our entry and set us on our new task. It was after dark and I was feeling really rough. I was on the bridge when a fierce pain hit me in the stomach and I doubled over with a groan. There was immediate consternation and the Sick Berth Attendant was called. These men are trained to treat the minor aches and pains of what is usually a fit bunch of individuals. Anything serious is immediately transferred to somewhere a doctor is available with all the necessary medical facilities. He diagnosed acute appendicitis, a diagnosis that subsequently proved correct.

The Captain immediately authorised a message to be sent requesting permission to enter harbour to drop off a seriously ill member of the ship's company. We could turn over the duty temporarily to the other escort, as there were only two ships involved in the new task. The reply came back not approving his request. This placed him in a real dilemma, as it was obvious I would have little chance of surviving without specialised help.

The tail end of the convoy had detached and was departing for Methil. He turned around and caught up with a sea going tug that was at the rear of the convoy. He asked him to come alongside, which he did They transferred me across to the tug but to this day I do not know how, I was far too ill to take any action but do as I was told. The people on the tug were kindness itself and put on all speed, overtook and passed the rest of the ingoing ships and tied up alongside within an hour.

An ambulance was waiting at the Jetty having been alerted by a signal from the tug. At first they though I was a merchant seaman and were taking me to the civilian hospital. This was corrected and they rushed me by road to a hospital set up especially for military casualties in a town called Bathgate outside Edinburgh. I was rushed in and prepared for surgery and at four in the morning was operated on by a Surgeon from Edinburgh University. He was apparently a famous surgeon and had been knighted for his services. I can no longer remember his name but when subsequent Doctors saw my medical file there were many raised eyebrows.

In the morning when I regained some semblance of consciousness he visited me and assured me that everything would be fine. He asked about the circumstances and when I told him he informed me I was very lucky to have a Captain who cared. He felt it would have been difficult for me indeed without the prompt attention. I certainly got the message. As this was a casualty hospital I had to be transferred immediately to a normal military hospital and it was here that things started to go very wrong.

The transport to take me to the other hospital turned out to be a van, there were no ambulances available. They laid me on the bottom of the van in an ordinary stretcher covered by a blanket. There was a soldier taking passage back to the hospital and he was perfectly mobile and climbed in the van after me. We took off and soon our speed increased to what was certainly the maximum road speed allowed.

As we turned corners I rolled almost off the stretcher and the young man did his best to keep me on the stretcher. We soon hit country roads and the twists turns and bumps made the ride a nightmare and the driver never eased up at all. The stretcher slid across the floor of the van, hitting the side and throwing me on to the floor. My fellow passenger did his best, he hammered at the front panel of the van trying to attract the drivers attention but it was no good. He wrestled me back on to the stretcher then braced his back against the side of the van in a sitting position and jammed his feet against the stretcher to try to keep it from moving.

In what turned out to be just over an hour but seemed like an eternity we pulled in front of a hospital. The doors opened and two orderlies started to slide me out of the van. When I was half way out I asked them to stop and looking up I asked where the driver was. The face of a WREN appeared and said cheerfully, “I was”. Never before or since have I used such language to a female. The young man who had been in the van with me joined in the invective. She was completely taken aback and by way of explanation she said that her normal duty was driving staff cars for officers. An Army Captain who turned out to be a doctor arrived on the scene and instructed the orderlies to get me inside.

They carried me in still covered in the blanket and laid it down alongside a bed. "Up you get in to bed" said the Captain. I couldn't believe this so I told him I couldn't the bandages were too tight. "What bandages" he asked. I really had to almost bite my tongue but before I could reply one of the orderlies pulled away the blanket. The smock I was wearing was supposed to be white but it was soaked in blood, the bandages were blood soaked and the stretcher had a pool where I was laying. I saw his face change colour, he practically screamed at the orderlies to get me into emergency. They cut off the bandages and of course the rough treatment had torn at the stitches and there was a steady trickle of blood.

An emergency call went out for the surgeon and an army major arrived and took over. They cleaned me up and he (very painfully I might add) repaired the damage. It turned out that they had their signals mixed and had prepared the operating room for an appendicitis case not knowing that the operation had been carried out. I was then taken to a ward where eleven other military men were being looked after. In that whole hospital there was only one naval man and that was I. In those days we had to always be accompanied by our gas masks, which in this case they hung at the end of the bed.

I had never encountered Army routine before and I suppose the way they performed was totally natural to them. Even though they were invalids, when they were mobile on crutches or walking painfully with the aid of a stick they would do their utmost to stand to attention and salute a passing officer. When the Sergeant in charge of the wards came through he would bark orders and rattle off routine instructions as if they were on a parade square. He had a bad habit of doing this at regular intervals from very early in the morning. When the army Doctors were doing their rounds he preceded them shouting at the top of his voice. It was inevitable that we would clash and we did.

It was early the second morning of my stay. I had slept fitfully on and off all the previous day and throughout the night I had to request painkillers from the orderly. I had just managed to get off into a deep sleep when this roaring voice penetrated my ears. "On gas masks", he was shouting, "For exercise on gas masks." He was standing quite near my bed and I sat half up and despite the fact it hurt like hell I told him in naval terms where he could go and what he could do with his gas mask.

Everyone in the ward heard me and from the far end came cries of support. Those nearest of course lay there quietly. The Sergeant, with a great show of efficiency, picked up my documents from the end of the bed then addressed me by my last name. "I am giving you a direct order," he said, "Put on your gas mask." I replied by telling him I had just given him a direct order in telling him what to do with his gas mask and he hadn't carried it out.

He was furious and went round checking to see that everyone else had their masks on; then after ordering them removed, he came back to my bed and told me I would be on the Commanding Officers report. I thanked him cheerfully and told him to go away. About ten minutes went by and I was just settling in to sleep when he was back again, this time with the Major. The Major asked me quite quietly if I had in fact said the things that the Sergeant reported and had I refused to put on the gas mask. I said yes. He asked me for an explanation and I told him that I had not slept, I was in pain, and the constant unnecessary shouting in a hospital ward made life for everyone very uncomfortable and was totally unnecessary.

The Major then asked how long I had been in the Army. I told him I wasn't in the Army; I was in the Navy. This caused some lifting of eyebrows, as this was strictly an Army hospital. He examined my documents closely and shook his head from side to side as if in sadness. The Sergeant said it did not make any difference, as it was a matter of military discipline and I had refused a direct order from a superior officer, I had used obscene language to a superior officer.

The Major asked me what a Yeoman was and when I explained, he turned to the Sergeant and suggested we drop the whole thing. The Sergeant protested but the Major pointed out that in a matter of rank the Sergeant was definitely not my superior officer. Apparently for purposes of discipline anyone who was a Sergeant or above was in a separate ward so they did not have to endure this endless screaming.

This exchange did cause a tremendous change. It was obvious that the Major who was a Doctor had not been fully aware of what had been going on and he had put a stop to it immediately. The Sergeant in the quiet of the next evening came and sat by my bed. He didn't make any excuses, none were necessary but it turned out his young brother was in the Navy. He wanted to know exactly what life was like. He told me where his brother was serving and he was delighted to hear it was a depot ship that never went to sea. He and I had no further problems.

The following day to my absolute astonishment the Coxswain arrived from the ship. The ship was alongside for two days and somehow he had wangled a car and driver from the motor pool and here he was. It was impossible to describe how I felt when I saw him and to make matters even better he opened a bag and inside was a carton of cigarettes and some chocolate bars. Cigarettes were in impossibly short supply ashore and the men in the ward strictly rationed themselves to two or three a day. We talked and I expressed my deepest fear that I would be replaced while I was in hospital. He told me that the First Lieutenant had anticipated the question and he could positively reassure me that I would return. They were borrowing a temporary replacement from the nearby depot ship.

Before he left he told me he had made the same car pool arrangements for tomorrow and a couple more would come down. When I heard this I asked him if they could bring more cigarettes for the rest of the ward, he agreed and they did. During my short stay there (eight days) that ward could have smoked themselves into oblivion. They were, I think, genuinely sorry to see me go as my visitors had gone all round and spent the day talking to each of them. I was given seven days sick leave and was back onboard a day before we had to sail on the next trip.

I had not intended to include this story, however; I have spent my life in the field of communications and I have never come to terms with the total misinterpretation that individuals can place on what seems to be a clear and straightforward message. I had access to the medical file (in fact I carried it back with me) so I looked up the message telling the hospital I was being sent. As far as I could read there was no room for the foul up as the message spelled out in clear terms what my status was. I asked the Sergeant and all became clear. The mailroom orderly on receipt of the message had phoned the Duty Officer and told him an appendicitis case was on its way. No details, then the message was filed.

CHAPTER EIGHTEEN

Search & Rescue

We arrived back in Rosyth and for the next two months or so we carried on with our usual business. Every trip was a nerve-wracking ordeal that, although we felt we knew every move, always seemed full of surprises. I would never have said this at the time, superstition would have prevented it, but we seemed to bear a charmed life. Actually it was not luck When men have been in action as a team under every condition the enemy can devise, their reaction to attack, their efficiency in dealing with it and above all their calm acceptance of a job to be done under difficult circumstances, odds improve on their side.

Throughout my life I have looked back in both awe and amazement at what these men achieved. To the permanent force men this was the task they had been trained for all their service life. They deserved praise I admit but the ones I take my hat off to were the officers and men who came straight from civilian life. My mind boggles at the thought of the transition they had to make and how efficiently and courageously they made it.

We had just tied up at the jetty in Rosyth in the middle of a blinding rainstorm. The visibility had been so bad coming up the Forth that there had been no chance for anyone to relax as we usually did after passing May Island on the homeward journey. We were all looking forward to a bath and a change of clothes and a quiet night in a still ship. A dispatch rider pulled up alongside the gangway that had just been put out. The rider was a WREN; they had taken over these duties and performed them admirably. She came onboard, handed me the packet of signals, which I signed for and took off in the rainstorm with a cheery wave.

Normally when arriving alongside, the postman would go to the Headquarters and pick up mail and the packet of signals. The fact that these had been delivered told me that there was some sort of priority message in the packet. Still in my oilskin and sea boots I went into the lobby and opened the packet. The first message I opened was the priority message, which started out with the ominous words: "Being in all respects ready to proceed you are etc., etc." I immediately went to the Captain's cabin and despite the fact that we had not been alongside more than twenty minutes he was spread out in a chair, still fully clothed in his sea going gear and fast asleep. I really felt terrible having to wake him but when I did he was as pleasant as ever with his "What have we got now Yeoman?"

The message was, as usual, terse and to the point. Top up with fuel and ammunition immediately and, when in all respects ready, proceed to a rendezvous point given in the message. A sealed package had arrived with the signals and the Captain opened it and read the contents. "My compliments to number one," he said, "ask him to see me as soon as convenient." The one thing I liked above all in the Royal Navy was the courtesy always displayed in what really was giving an order. Everything was requested, suggested, as convenient or if possible. This applied from the Captain downwards and made life much more pleasant.

I told the First Lieutenant and then carried on forward to warn the Coxswain. I couldn't tell him the reason, I simply did not know, but I knew we would not be alongside long enough to go through our usual routine. He was busy changing in the mess when I came in and when he saw my face he stopped, "What's up Yeo." I told him we would be moving and as I spoke, the pipe "Special sea duty men close up" was heard throughout the ship. This pipe is the harbinger of going to sea and the mutterings and grumbling could be heard everywhere. I was still in my sea going rig so I went directly up to the Bridge. The Coxswain followed me up the ladder on his way to the wheelhouse to take over the wheel. This was his duty leaving harbour, going alongside or in action or in any emergency that required rapid manoeuvres.

We cast off and went alongside the oiler that was expecting us. The ammunition lighter came alongside and we topped up on the ammunition we had expended on our last run. It always struck me that in these emergencies no authority thought of sending out a lighter with food. There were so many occasions we had sailed in a hurry and never had provisions treated as if they were important. I do remember one occasion when we had, due to emergencies, run completely out of food except for biscuits. We didn't even have a tin of normally ever-present pilchards or sausage.

When we arrived at our destination, we were immediately turned around to oil and ammunition and sail. The Captain made a signal requesting that provisions be sent out. He was told that only ammunition would be sent. His reply was "Food is an ammunition of war, please comply". We received the provisions, but the Captain was requested to put his reasons in writing for declining to sail without the provision lighter. I understand when his reply was received the base supply officer had to put his reasons in writing to the Admiral why he had not been briefed on the state of our food supply.

After we had completed everything with the rain still pouring down we headed back down the Forth for our rendezvous. We were briefed by the Captain and it turned out we were to rendezvous with a group of destroyers to carry out an extended sweep towards Norway to locate ships that had escaped from Norwegian ports after they had been caught in the harbours by the Germans. They had placed guards onboard and removed most of the crew except the minimum necessary to maintain the ship and, if necessary, move her in the anchorage.

This is one operation, except for the stories told to me by the survivors, about which I could never find any official documentation to give me the complete picture. However what I heard and saw was quite enough to convince me that an operation requiring tremendous courage and audacity had been carried out both by naval personnel and men of the merchant navy.

We rendezvoused with five other destroyers, all Hunt class modern destroyers. The Captain (D) in charge ordered us to the very end of the line. There was at least two miles between each ship in line abreast. We were the real old timer and I had a feeling that, despite the fact that our Captain was among the most senior, the Captain (D) did not want his nice looking flotilla marred by our presence among them. We were told to increase speed to 25 knots which we all did and kept a steady line into a very calm sea.

After an hour at this speed a message was passed through all the other destroyers addressed to us asking us if we could maintain this speed. The Captain did not like it and expressed his displeasure. The Wallace had four boilers and was capable of 33 knots on all boilers. On three boilers she could do 29 knots with ease. We knew the maximum speed of the Hunt class modern destroyers was 28 and the navy always required that ships would always be held to 2 knots below the maximum for manoeuvring safety. He told me to make the reply that there was no problem in maintaining this speed. However I had an idea, having heard him express his annoyance.

I suggested we ask the Captain (D) if 25 knots would be the maximum speed for the search. The Captain was a bit puzzled and asked me why. I said that if he came back and said yes, which we knew he would, we would then hoist the signal flags which would have to be repeated by all ships up to Captain (D), request permission to die out boilers not required. He roared with laughter and that is exactly what we did. When the Captain (D) received the message, he passed a reply down the line in which he quoted from Proverbs a sentence that conveyed a sincere apology.

We steamed throughout the night and the day dawned with a brilliant morning and flat calm sea. We saw the first of the ships but the enemy had got there first and a torpedo launched from an aircraft had blown a huge hole in her starboard side. The torpedo must have hit before it hit the water as the hole was above the water line and she was, at the moment, not in danger of sinking. The crew was in the process of abandoning ship and we circled her while the others carried on with the search.

We heard the Lookout, "Aircraft bearing 090, low down"; we all switched our binoculars to that bearing except the two, who since our unexpected high bomber attack were always scanning the skies for the unexpected. The aircraft were torpedo bombers complete with floats. (Later the Coxswain would comment that they were coming in sea boots now). They came towards us and, after the air attacks we were used to, they seemed to be very slow. The order to open fire was given and I don't know what the pilots expected but, at the first burst of gunfire around them, they turned and headed back towards the coast.

While we stood guard and circled, one of the other destroyers closed and picked up the survivors. We recommenced the search but in every case the Germans had got there first and there was either debris and survivors or a sinking ship. It was heartbreaking after such a courageous and well-planned operation. The story of the operation was that several ships, some Norwegian and some British, full of cargoes destined for Britain had been caught in the Norwegian harbours. As I have said, the Germans put the guards onboard but the Navy conceived a plan to smuggle a small group of men to each ship. Their task was to overpower the guards, raise steam and sail where a group of Destroyers would be waiting for them.

Using submarines and, with the aid of the Norwegian resistance, the first part of the plan had worked well. Ten ships had been taken over simultaneously and sailed in the middle of the night. The German occupation was not many weeks in place and the Norwegian resistance had already a framework in place to assist the allies. They felt that the element of surprise would work in our favour in getting out of the ports. This proved to be true and they all managed to get on the high seas. The tragedy was that we were too late getting there and they were helpless targets to the torpedo bombers and other aircraft attacks. Why the rescue flotilla was late I will never know. I often wondered if the lack of documentation of this action was due to the fact that someone in high places fouled it up.

We were detached and told to return to Rosyth, which we did, and breathed a sigh of relief when we pulled alongside. Our relief was short lived, the dispatch rider arrived delivered her packet and left. I opened it and there it was again. The Captain wasn't asleep, he was spread out on his armchair when I walked in. I showed him the message and this time there was no time for fuel (at his discretion of course), we had to proceed with all dispatch through the mine barrier to escort a merchant ship seen heading for the barrier by our reconnaissance aircraft.

We were underway in less than half an hour. It was just after dark and keeping to the legal limit for passage down the Forth a very disgruntled ship's company settled in for another unexpected and totally unwelcome trip. After May Island the navigator very carefully planned our course. The mine barrier was a continuous mine field laid by the Navy all down the coast to prevent incursion by the enemy, particularly U boats, into the coastal waters. They could wreak havoc if they could get through. It did mean, however, that our navigation had to be accurate in order to pass through the channels that had been left to enable our own ships to pass through. The secret of these channels was very closely guarded.

We passed through the mine barrier without incident and proceeded in the direction needed to intercept the ship that had been sighted. We found him almost immediately. He was heading straight for the coast and was less than an hours' steaming from the mine barrier. On the course he was heading he would not have survived. Signalling with a shaded light, we instructed him to follow closely in our wake. The ship was less than a thousand tons with a maximum speed of 11 knots. We reversed our course and plodded through the night, to arrive safely in the entrance to the Forth at daylight where we could have a good look at our find.

He was one of the ships that had escaped from Norway and apparently had lived a charmed life as, at no time, had the enemy spotted him. He came alongside in Rosyth and it was from the crew we learned of this remarkable operation. His cargo was diamond-cutting tools, a desperately needed item for the factories turning out war material. It was with some hesitation we decided to go into our harbour routine, but there were no more alarms and excursions so for the first time in over two weeks we could take our clothes off, bathe and relax.

CHAPTER NINETEEN

Out of Luck

We had been running the gauntlet for almost two years before our luck ran out. We were heading north with the usual complement of ships and had reached the narrow channel just south of Folkestone. We were as usual the lead escort and we had just steamed up the convoy between the convoy and the shore trying to get one ship from constantly breaking the column. Apparently he had some problems with his steering but it was now fixed. We were about four ships from the head of the convoy when a group of six bombers escorted by two fighters came in to attack. We opened fire above the ships lying between ourselves and the bombers and increased speed to the maximum to get clear of the convoy where we could act more freely.

At this moment I stepped down from the compass platform itself onto the bridge. I picked up the VHF radio and contacted the fighters that were on patrol in the area. I received a reply from them, logged the time and stepped back onto the platform. To my astonishment we were blanketed in thick white fog. We could hear the crump of bombs but it was impossible to see a target. We were still moving at full speed to get clear of the ships and now, if possible, the low-lying fog we had suddenly encountered.

Thinking we were now clear of the column of ships the Captain ordered a turn to starboard. We started to turn when one of the lookouts screamed, "Ship to starboard". It was too late and out of the fog came the leader of the column who had increased speed to twice the speed of the convoy to get clear of the fog. His increased speed led to the miscalculation and he rammed us amidships with an enormous crash.

Men in the boiler room where his bows hit died. Except for a bent bow he had no casualties. The bombing was continuing as the bombers could see the masts of the ships above the low lying fog. We were effectively sitting ducks. Now we had to save the ship, try and get a shot at the bombers while our damage control team went to work shoring up bulkheads. The fog cleared as rapidly as it had arrived and we could put up a defence for the convoy. There was a call through the loudspeaker from the aircraft, "Tally ho," and no call ever sounded sweeter as the fighters signalled they had seen and were chasing the enemy.

The ship was visibly settling as loads of water poured in through the enormous hole in the side. The Captain instructed me to pass a signal by radio giving our position and I called it down to the radio room. Unknown to me the radio room was already flooding with oil filled water and the P.O.Tel had sent his staff out of there and on to the upper deck. He made the signal and stayed there listening for any calls.

The damage control team had managed to shore up the bulkheads between the torn compartments and the rest of the ship. All watertight doors were in place with the majority of the ship's company except the engine room staff on the upper deck. The ship had settled considerably with the upper deck not far from the ocean level but we were holding our own. Later it was observed officially that the reaction and training of the damage control crew must have been of the highest order to save the ship under such circumstances.

We were fortunate in that a sea going tug was the designated rescue ship of the convoy. Within a very short time we were made fast alongside him and in this manner made our way back to the Thames and to the dry dock in Tilbury. When we arrived and were tied up in the dry dock and the dock had been drained the Coxswain asked for volunteers to go down and bring up the dead. Naturally all the stokers volunteered, as these were their messmates. It was a sad time and there was little conversation or discussion went on that day.

We thought that being as severely damaged as we were they would pay the ship off and bring in a new crew when she was repaired. This was the normal routine but we prayed that this would not happen, as it would be like taking a superbly trained team and splitting them up one by one all over the fleet.

It was at this time the influence of our Captain in high places took over. The instructions had already been drafted to pay the ship off but before they could be issued he was on his way to Admiralty. The ship was habitable having been pumped out and cleaned out by the ships company and a host of dockyard workmen. The damage was already being assessed and plans for repair were in the works.

It turned out that the repairs could be completed in two weeks and within that time frame all the other outstanding items could be carried out. There was one problem; the ship was an old timer and the plates had to be riveted; they could not be welded. In those days hand riveting was rarely done. The dockyard foreman however said he knew where a team could be put together of old timers who could do the job and this was arranged.

To our entire delight, although mine was short lived, the ship's company were sent on leave for ten days except for a very few care and maintenance people. These were drawn from volunteers who all lived in London and district and could get home every night they were free. I was preparing to go, in fact I had my railway warrant and ration cards when the Captain sent me for. He showed me a letter he had received which instructed him to send me on a special course to H.M.S. Mercury, the signal school that was housed in a mansion once belonging to Beatrice Lillie the actress who had donated it to the war effort. It was situated way out in the country in a place called Leydene. The village nearby was the first place that cricket was ever played.

To say I was upset would be to put it mildly; I was furious and couldn't possibly conceive of any course that was important enough to cancel my well-earned leave. The Captain told me he had called the school to determine why. He said that they would not discuss it on the telephone except to say it was essential for the new equipment being fitted while we were in dock.

I took off with ill grace and spent the next few days listening to lectures on Radio Detection Finding (RDF) and looking at a small cathode ray tube with a green line running across it, which looked like fuzzy grass. This of course was the early Radar set fitted to ships. They were sending two specially trained operators with this equipment, which incidentally at this time was highly secret. I failed to understand why I had been sent. This was more in the line of the P.O.Telegraphist or the electronics maintenance people. I asked but was never enlightened.

The two specially trained operators we eventually received were rated as able seaman and carried in the communication mess where they made themselves thoroughly unpopular. It turned out that these two were actors in training from a London theatre school and had already appeared as young leading men in some plays. Their speech and accent was imitation officer. They were convinced that their present rank was a grave mistake and made this quite clear.

I returned to the ship half way through the repair period. The Chief Boatswains Mate was delighted to see me. He lived in London and had been keeping a duty watch every second day. Now, with me there he knew I would stand in for him leaving his nights free to go home. He gave me a quick turn over about fire alarms and all the other essentials. There were only two men in the watch and they were allowed ashore in the evening. The ship's galley was closed and all over the deck were the power cables, gas hoses, water hoses and all the dozens of things the dockyard workers left in position when they stopped for the day. He told me there was only one officer onboard, a new sub lieutenant called Prince. He had joined the ship two days ago and seemed like a nice enough fellow.

After he left I went down to the wardroom to look for this new Sub. I found him reading a newspaper and when I went in and introduced myself he shook hands and welcomed me back onboard. He was taller than I and had blond hair with very blue eyes and a somewhat prominent thin nose. I supposed women would find him attractive, later I found my supposition was quite correct. We sat and talked and it was obvious that he was even younger than I was. His last ship had been the Valiant, a battleship and he said he was really looking forward to being in a destroyer. We exchanged experiences for a time and of course he was interested in what we had been doing and what had happened.

It was late in the evening and time for us to get something to eat. I suggested going to a pub just near the docks, he could go first and when he returned I would go. He suggested instead we make supper onboard. I agreed but pointed out that my mess forward was uninhabitable and the duty Petty Officer (which tonight was myself) was using a hammock in the after lobby. I had been left a bunch of sandwiches by the one I had relieved as the ships galley was out of action. He invited me to have supper with him in the wardroom so together we foraged and found some sausages, some powdered egg, potatoes and a can of brown beans. I hope he still remembers that meal because in the light of future events I certainly do.

We had it all nicely cooked and with some bread we had found and tea we had made we settled in to have a meal. We had not started when the wardroom door opened and Sub Lieut. Smith (the bane of my life) entered with another sub and two giggling young ladies. He saw me sitting at the table and I could see his eyes light up at the thought of ordering me out of the wardroom or making some other derogatory remarks. Just then Sub Lieut. Prince gestured for him to come over which he did. In a very quiet voice he told him the ship was not open to visitors, also we were eating. To my absolute astonishment, Smith gathered up his companion and left practically pushing the two young women ahead of them.

We carried on with our supper during which he asked about the ship in general. He never, however, mentioned or asked about the Captain or other officers and I really appreciated his adherence to this protocol. Despite the curiosity he must have had about the Captain and officers he was going to serve with he would not ask a Petty Officer about the officers. We had a very pleasant evening and it was quite late when we finally decided to call it a day.

The next morning the Captain arrived onboard about ten o'clock. I took him all the outstanding signals and he asked about the course. I described to him the equipment they were at this moment fitting and we both hoped it would do what had been promised. The idea of being able to detect aircraft before they could see you and know which direction they were coming from sounded too good to be true.

He then asked if I had met the new Sub. I told him about the previous evening and the meal we had put together. I added that I found the new Sub very pleasant indeed to talk to and he seemed to have some war experience. He then told me that the new Sub was H.R.H. Prince Philip of Greece and Denmark. I understood now why the Sub Lieut. Smith had beaten such a hasty retreat; he wanted to start off with a good impression.

There were a few days left before we were supposed to be ready to sail again. I requested permission to go on leave for those few days, which was granted. I spent it in my home town of Bradford in Yorkshire and it was on this leave I met the girl with whom I was destined to spend most of my life with although, naturally at the time I had no idea. I returned to the ship after five days and we promised to write to each other. A promise we both kept and for the first time in my life I was looking for the mail to arrive.

We returned to our usual task of East Coast convoys with the occasional foray into some overnight or two day operation. Weeks turned into months and the deadly battle continued without respite. We had no formal leave; the only break was when we had to stay in for five days to get the boilers cleaned. The ship's company took turns to go on leave so we looked forward with great anticipation for our turn to come.

CHAPTER TWENTY

Royalty to be

Here I must digress. The enormous interest people display when they learn that I served and was in close contact with Prince Philip for such a long time and under the most difficult conditions leads to a host of questions. I will try to satisfy their curiosity and at the same time I hope I can convey something of his character.

As I have said, he was quite tall, blond haired, had an aquiline nose, very blue eyes, and by any standard was good looking. When he joined the ship he was an acting sub Lieutenant having just passed his qualifying examinations for that rank. He had already seen war service in the Ramillies (battleship), Kent (cruiser) Valiant (battleship) as a midshipman. He was mentioned in dispatches for his services onboard Valiant during the battle of Matapan in early 1941. His citation was for manning the searchlights during the battle; but I doubt if it had been just another midshipman the citation would have existed.

I make this comment not to downgrade his efforts but to illustrate the tremendous difficulties he laboured under. His Uncle Lord Louis Mountbatten pulled every string humanly possible to ensure that Philip had smooth sailing in his career. I don't say chosen career because I once heard him express his deep admiration for the Air Force and I certainly received the impression that at sometime his heart had pulled him in that direction. With Mountbatten in the background making requests of senior commanders and Admirals to find useful employment for Philip it was obvious that anything they did was more to ingratiate themselves with Mountbatten than to further Philip's career. This made it difficult for him

It is a fact that he needed no such help. He was dedicated to his profession, totally capable and his personality was such that the "Royal" business never came through either in work or conversation. Stories have been told about how women swooned over him and every woman with an unmarried daughter made every effort to attract his attention. How all the WRENS in the base at Rosyth tried their best to catch his eye and how he was always seen in the company of the most gorgeous women. How he was secretly engaged in those days to the lady who is now our Queen. I think most people forget the basic facts. He was only 18 almost 19 when he joined the Wallace. The queen was then 13 and it would have been a miracle if such an engagement ever existed. All these stories were simply hot air.

There is no question that when visiting Australia and other places in his previous ships he was entertained most royally and was photographed with attractive partners. Some of these photographs surfaced among the ship's company and were pinned on the notice board with comments such as "Nice work if you can get it," etc., and when he saw them he laughed as much as anyone.

The fact that when he could he visited the Royal Family is very obvious. Mountbatten was welcome at the palace and so by extension was his nephew. However, as I have said, during these visits the present Queen and her sister were school children and some time had to pass before their ages were such that serious thought to an alliance was possible. This was after he left the Wallace.

In the still watches of the night he was a pleasure to talk to. His early training had been very tough but very fair (unlike the Ganges) but it was obvious he was a physical doer not an academic. His spelling left a great deal to be desired but his instant grasp of a tactical and dangerous situation certainly saved the ship on one occasion. Despite his young age he made the other sub lieutenants look like rank amateurs, which of course they were. He was a Greek citizen although a more English person in speech and mannerisms would be difficult to find. On one occasion when we were trying to persuade a Greek ship to get back in the column over the loudspeaker and the Greek Captain indicating he did not understand, our Captain sent for Philip to act as interpreter. To his astonishment and I must admit to mine, he professed to be unable to speak Greek enough to help. He had been away from the language from a very young age.

During his time in the Wallace he never had the privilege of a days leave more than any one of the ship's company and officers. As I have said, our leave time was very restricted but despite this he never made an effort to get extra time ashore. I remember one time in London alongside the dock he was duty officer and I was going ashore. He asked me to send a cable for him, which I did; he wouldn't even leave the ship to do that bit of personal business. Incidentally, a long time afterwards I found the original of the cable in my notebook with a note that he owed me five shillings. He still does.

He was extremely thoughtful and very courteous. I treasure a telegram he sent with the other officers wishing me well on my wedding day. When my wife met him she fell under the spell of his old world courtesy. On occasions we shared a taxi together from the ship to the railway station and I felt clumsy at the way he could make my wife feel as if, at that moment, she was the most important person in the world.

Despite the fact that he was officially a Greek citizen and, under the rules, could not be promoted above his sub lieutenant rank until he was a British citizen, it became obvious that he was head and shoulders above his contemporaries. Something had to be done and with the strongest possible recommendations from our Captain and of course the background pushing of Mountbatten the condition was waived and he became the youngest Lieutenant in the Royal Navy who at the same time was the first Lieutenant of a Destroyer. It is rare for a ship's company to be interested in the promotion of the officers but this was a very popular move with them. For the record he did not become a British citizen until 1947.

I have had the pleasure of meeting him again several times during his visits to different places. It is difficult to describe the feeling of nostalgia when we exchange a few word of reminiscence. I sincerely admire him for his courage, his dignity and above all for his total down to earth approach with everyone irrespective of their (so called) social standing.

It wasn't long after we had completed repairs and sailed that at a clear lower deck ceremony (this is where the whole ship's company is mustered to be informed of something that affects them all). They were usually, in these days, the forecaster of trying times to come. This was not the case this time. The Captain informed us that he had been awarded the "Distinguished Service Order" (D.S.O.). We cheered and really meant it, he was, in all ways, a dedicated and efficient officer who took great pains to ensure the ship's company were thoroughly considered at all times.

I hate to bring a sour note into a merited award but during his speech he told the ship's company that the honour was as much theirs as his, and he meant it. A voice muttered in the background, yes, but who will wear the ribbon. He of course did not hear it but it was obvious that the voice was echoing the sentiments of many.

I have always considered the method of awarding decorations in the Royal Navy to be not only ridiculous but a method of perpetuating rank snobbery. By this I mean that, if an officer is award a decoration for performing the identical act that a rating performs, his decoration is termed an "Order", the rating receives a medal. We therefor find the "D.S.O." becomes for the rating a "D.S.M.", a much less coveted award. This applies to all the decorations except the Victoria Cross. Where the Captain of a ship is awarded a decoration, as in this case, the whole ship's company has earned it but they cannot wear a ribbon or any indication of this fact.

It is a common sight to see senior officers with so many ribbons they have difficulty putting them on so the public can see them all. Except for those that have been awarded for an individual act of bravery, and these are few, the rest are for just being there like the stars we give to children for attending classes promptly or being toilet trained at an early age. There is not a single Admiral or General who does not owe every decoration he has to the men that serve him yet they walk away with nothing.

As an example of the careful consideration given to awarding decorations to ratings the following is absolutely true. A Yeoman, who distinguished himself at the evacuation and was recommended for a decoration along with other members of the ship's company, left the ship before the awards were made by Admiralty. He was disgusted to learn that the Yeoman who relieved him, who, during the evacuation, had been in Barracks ashore, was awarded the D.S.M. for his services on that ship during the evacuation. He complained, the situation was confirmed but nothing could be done about it.

Admiralty had awarded the decorations based on an incorrect list that had been requested some time after the Yeoman left and never bothered to check if the list represented those who were actually there Until this scheme of awarding unequal decorations for identical service is corrected the class distinction will continue to exist along with the unpleasant snobbery that goes with it. As for the floral mish mash worn by Senior Officers, if they really knew the ridicule that was heaped on them by the men who really earn the decorations they would think twice before accepting them.

It was not long after this that the Captain was transferred to other duties ashore an appointment that was richly deserved. It was, however, a considerable blow to the ship's company and to myself in particular. I went through all the anticipated horror situations in my mind and for days I wasn't fit to talk to.

In the Chief and Petty Officers mess, in order to pass such spare time that we had (not much) the Coxswain had proposed that we build a scale model of the ship. Each member of the mess was given a task that suited his particular part of ship (for example I had the signal lanterns and small flags). These were combined by the Coxswain and the Shipwright, and other willing hands, into a superb model. When it was finished it was put on display but when the Captain, who had greatly admired it, was due to leave we gave it to him. I will never forget his face, there were tears in his eyes as he accepted and said goodbye. Incidentally, these many years have passed and I know he died but I have never been able to trace what happened to the model. I expect it is in some museum somewhere but the story of its origin will be lost.

The new Captain was a Lieutenant with, of course, several years experience. He knew that he could never fill the boots of the man who had left and he did not try. He rapidly became familiar with the Chief and Petty Officers and the bridge personnel. He treated me exactly as his predecessor had treated me and it was not long before we established the rapport necessary to feel comfortable. After a few weeks onboard however, I detected a very cold atmosphere between him and the other officers. There was none of the usual joking camaraderie that had been the tenor of life on the bridge between the Captain and the officers. Even Philip, who was normally irrepressible, seemed to act more formally in his presence. The Captain's attitude to me never changed and I have to confess I rather liked him and was puzzled by the atmosphere. I never did find out the cause of the coldness.

CHAPTER TWENTY-ONE

Marriage

My long distance courtship had proceeded extremely well. Every mail brought letters and I must admit that I had not realised what I had been missing in the overall scheme of things. For the first time life outside the influence of the Navy had an impact on my thinking. We numbered our letters to each other in order to be certain we received them all. It was an advantage, as the mail chased us all over, and we would receive letters completely out of sequence and know that somewhere, floating around, were the missing numbers. It was possible to be able to explain that a reply to a specific question had not been made or a comment on a subject had not been done simply because we had not received the letter containing the query or subject.

We had been in for boiler cleaning a few times and during the leave made possible by these spells alongside we had come to know each other very well. I had determined when the war was over that I would ask her to marry me. I thought life was far too hazardous to inflict such a worry on her. She argued vehemently against this saying that there was no forecast when the war would be over and, in any case, we had every right to start on our future together and accept the risk. I describe this state of our relationship to explain what was to follow.

It was May 1943 and messages were arriving by hand when alongside and encrypted when we were at sea. They were all highly classified and, in theory should have been known to only the Captain and the Cypher officer. Our cypher officer had not changed and he had enormous difficulty grappling with the messages. Some of them were in systems he did not know existed and repeatedly I had to give him a hand to break them down. The Captain was fully aware of this and when the Sub produced the plain language version he would pointedly thank me as well. It was obvious a massive operation was being planned of which we were to become a part. The occasional sentences that I could not help but see indicated that the operation would be in a hot climate and require extensive sea time with fuelling and provisioning at sea when necessary. The code word Husky was used to identify the messages and the operation. At no time was the specific nature of the operation defined and the date was in very general terms.

As the saying goes "A wink is as good as a nod to a blind horse" and no wink or nod was allowed to the ship's company. I determined to take advantage of my knowledge and in my next letter suggested that during my next boiler cleaning leave, at the beginning of June, we should get married. I had memories of the Devonshire where an absence of two years was taken for granted by the Navy. I later learned that this letter threw everyone, particularly my future wife, into a state of chaos. To me it merely represented taking a couple of hours to go to the nearest registry office to get married by the Registrar. No big deal as long as the license was in order this my future wife was obtaining. Of course this was my first lesson in learning how obtuse men are when it comes to the finer points in life.

I arrived home to find that all sorts of things had been arranged down to the car that would take us to the Registry office (not easy with the shortage and rationing of petrol.) Accommodation had been booked at a lovely hotel in the Yorkshire Moors for our very brief (two day) honeymoon. Food had been arranged and guests, some of whom I had never met, had been invited to the house for celebrations after the wedding.

Telegrams started to arrive from my shipmates as I had announced my intentions before going on leave. Among these was the one I referred to including Philip. I must admit I never mentioned this at the wedding as, both my new wife and I hated the idea of name-dropping among our guests and friends. There were doomsayers among both family and friends. "Marry in haste, repent at leisure," was an oft quoted remark both light-heartedly and seriously. I wish I could see them now. Over fifty years our marriage lasted and blessed us with four wonderful daughters. They in their turn brought the blessings of many grandchildren and now even great grandchildren. I hope the doomsayers' long planned and carefully considered marriages gave them the same happiness.

When I returned I, of course, had to endure the ribald remarks and double-edged jokes that always follows these occasions. I was again fortunate in that the Rosyth area was near my wife's birthplace so in the short time before sailing she came up to visit on several occasions. She was entertained onboard for meals many times and grew to know and like the men with whom I had lived closely for so long. The feeling was mutual and always after, when the mail arrived, I would be asked how she was doing with reminders to remember them to her, which I always did.

The Coxswain had got wind of something in the offing. He quizzed me unmercifully but in all honesty I could not add to what he suspected. He did not believe me but didn't hold it against me; he knew the problem I had. He decided however to make some preparations of his own for a long sea trip. He didn't know where but he knew that any long trip would mean running out of fresh provisions very quickly. He came up with the idea of buying some wooden buckets and preserving beef in one, pork in another and mutton in another. In this way, when the fresh meat ran out after the usual four days we could fall back on fresh roasts instead of the interminable tinned sausage and pilchards.

He, being raised on a farm in the days of no refrigeration, was familiar with the technique. We all agreed and when the fresh provisions were issued just prior to sailing he insisted that additional roasts be issued to the Chief and P.O.'s mess. It was useless trying to add more for the ship's company or officers; there simply was no way of preserving such an amount. We did not realise it at the time but we were building up a real morale problem.

We sailed south to link up with a small force of destroyers. We came under the orders of a Captain (D) who formed the flotilla into a single line and we set off to some (to us) undisclosed rendezvous. We went to routine action stations just before dawn and when dawn broke there was an incredible sight. As far as the eye could see were merchant ships formed in the largest convoy that ever sailed. I learned later that there were well over a thousand ships assembling for this operation and what we could see was only a small portion of them. They were carrying some 3,000 Landing Craft and hundreds of thousands of troops.

We plodded on for days through the Bay of Biscay and passed through the Straits of Gibralter at night. We had to go alongside the jetty in Gibraltar to fuel and provision and during this a saboteur blew up several tanks of high-octane fuel just as we were about to pull alongside. We backed off hurriedly without casualties; he had exploded the bomb too early. Through the binoculars we could see the culprit running along the jetty to escape but unfortunately for him, an alert sentry spotted him, ordered him to halt and when he tried to dodge away shot him. We went alongside another jetty without further incident. On completion we sailed to rejoin the main body of ships.

The Germans were well informed of the goings and comings in and around Gibraltar and the infamous British traitor known as "Lord Haw Haw" included the name of our ship in his next broadcast. The famous ruse of the corpse of a dead British officer floating ashore in Spain with the plans for the invasion of Greece and Sardinia certainly paid off. The Germans were obviously aware of the large number of ships heading in and through the Mediterranean but all their defences were in Greece and Sardinia. We learned later that Hitler only approved a small contingent to back up the defences of Sicily and even they were told not to rely on the Italians if anything did occur.

We had run out of fresh meat and were back on the tinned sausage etc. It was decided to roast half of one of the joints. We picked the beef. The smell of roasting beef permeated the galley and drifted down to the mess deck. We were sitting down to eat when the mess man came to the Coxswain saying a Leading Hand from each mess was waiting to see him. He was quite startled and went out to see what the problem was. They asked to be taken to see the Captain to state a complaint. This was as near a mutiny as could be and the Coxswain, well known for his fairness was terribly upset. It turned out that their complaint was of unfair treatment in that the Chiefs and Petty Officers had fresh meat and they had only tinned stuff.

He brought them all into the mess and told them what he had done and it was strictly a mess arranged thing and had nothing to do with the overall supplies for the ship. While they understood they couldn't get it out of their minds that in some way they had been badly treated. They had to explain it to their individual messmates and it would be hard to convince them that they had not been short changed.

It was a real dilemma; we could not possibly afford this type of feeling to permeate the ship. The Coxswain, as usual, came up with a solution. There was just over twenty pounds of meat in each bucket except the beef, which had been reduced by about five pounds. He suggested to the Leading Hands that they take the pork and the mutton totalling forty pounds. He pointed out that if they were both cooked at the same time there would be, after cooking, at least a quarter of a pound for each man. They could arrange that all the mess members would be made aware of exactly what had happened and in future make their own salting down arrangements.

The incident passed without anyone other than the people involved being aware of the possible consequences that could have occurred. It certainly taught every Chief and Petty Officer a lesson in the delicate balance that has to be maintained to ensure that even if what you do is correct it has also to be perceived to be correct. We sat around and discussed the situation that had quite innocently arisen and finally admitted we had been very short-sighted. The following night the Officer of the Watch, in a too casual enquiry, spoke about the delicious smell that had come from the Galley that day. I agreed with him and commented that they must have found a new way to cook tinned sausages.

CHAPTER TWENTY-TWO

Invasion Sicily

It was the 8th of July 1943 and the largest Armada of ships ever put together was all around us. They plodded on and we ran around them listening, looking and let's face it, praying. We knew now what a precious cargo those ships contained, over 150 thousand men and landing craft. It was the Navy's responsibility to get them to the beaches of Sicily and make sure by our vigilance that the enemy could not stop them. Overhead the fighters patrolled in what seemed to be an endless stream; a heartening sight.

That day passed uneventfully and we found it difficult to believe that the enemy seemed unaware of our presence. On the last day before the actual invasion we could detect all sorts of activity going on onboard the ships as we passed them. Landing craft were being readied to lower, soldiers seemed to be massing on the upper decks, probably for last minute briefings and a couple of high speed motor launches were making their way in and out of the columns. Probably passing on last minute information and orders. One had come alongside us and passed over an envelope, which was taken below by our Cypher officer.

Just before sunset our senior officer had ordered us to hoist battle ensigns. These were the largest ensigns carried in the ship and were flown from the masthead. The theory was that we could be readily identified by our own forces. By the same token, of course, we could readily be identified by the enemy. The battle ensign, which I had flown a few times, was a nuisance. As the ship moved around and reversed course etc, it became wrapped around the mast and we had to have a signalman constantly trying to clear it instead of doing his proper job. There was tremendous tension in the ship. We all knew that at dawn we would be into a battle situation that we simply had no experience with and we had no idea what to expect.

At times like these the senior officers try to manufacture a legend about themselves and the battle to come. This senior officer of the Destroyers was no exception and I spent a difficult and useless half hour reading a signal his ship was sending by light to each of us. We were moving at speed, the sea was running a bit and the light was very small. At first I thought that some vital message to do with the operation was going to be passed and strained to read every word. I remember the opening sentence to this day, it was, "On this the eve of the largest sea borne invasion the world has ever known", it then went on to a long diatribe about courage, efficiency, the world is watching etc., etc. It was this officer's version of Nelson's famous signal but it was wrapped in useless verbiage and platitudes. The message never survived to surface again at some later date thank goodness.

The dawn arrived and already we could see the Landing craft leaving their mother ships. Ahead of them and nearer the beaches were a series of Landing Craft of a type I had never seen before. I soon found out their function as they opened fire. They were rocket ships with rows and rows of rockets that blazed skywards towards the beaches in a reMorseless barricade. For a moment I felt a sense of horror as all along the beach turned into a sea of flame. Every destroyer opened fire with a barrage laid down on the beaches and as the Landing craft approached the beach with the invading soldiers the barricade intensified until I could have sworn that there could not be one survivor. Of course this was wishful thinking.

At that moment the enemies shore batteries opened up on the ships over the heads of the Landing Craft. We turned and still firing started to Zig Zag. I saw two flags hoisted on the senior officers ship, I could see clearly what they were but I had no idea what they meant and I reported my failure to the Captain who was very annoyed. Suddenly he said, "Check with Smith, an envelope came onboard this morning." Smith was at the back of the bridge when I rushed up to him and demanded if he had received any new signal orders.

He reached in his back pocket and pulled out a sheet of paper. He told me that this had arrived but it was only amendments to the signal books that could wait. I opened it and there in large print was the name "Operation Husky" and underneath it a series of two letter emergency signals that could be used as not everyone had the naval signal books. I could have hit him. The signal flying meant make smoke and I rushed the answering pendant to the top and informed the Captain of the meaning. The signal was executed and we put up an intense smoke barrier between the ships and the shore. What transpired between the Captain and Smith over this incident I never knew but it certainly did nothing to improve our relationship.

Since, naturally, the invasion of Normandy overshadows any other sea borne invasion, it is not generally known that the invasion of Sicily committed more men, more ships and more aircraft than the

Normandy invasion. At one time there were over a thousand allied aircraft, a thousand ships carrying troops, they landed in the first waves 150 thousand men and eventually committed three million men to this invasion of Sicily and Italy.

Naturally the day was spent in acute anticipation. From what we could see things were going well for the British and Canadian troops but the radio communication was telling us a different story about the American troops. The full story of this is now well documented in official archives so I must limit myself to what I could see and hear. We heard the army artillery spotters calling for firepower in different locations and the Navy would respond with heavy gunfire. It was a tremendous boost to hear the Army spotters call in that the target they wanted eliminated had been dealt with.

We had the monitor HMS Lord Roberts in the harbour now. She had a twin turret of fifteen-inch guns that could place a shell weighing a ton accurately on a target 20 miles away. Late in the afternoon we heard an Army Spotter calling for fire power several miles away. The troops were being held down by intense enemy action at some difficult terrain. The Lord Roberts guns slowly swung around and each barrel moving up and down independently until it seemed that they had both decided on the correct angle.

The whole ship seemed to explode and move backwards in the water as the shells were fired. Not many seconds later over the radio we heard the Army Spotter and he could not keep the incredulous amazement out of his voice. Instead of reporting the fall of shot in true military manner he practically screamed, "They have gone, they have gone, what the hell was that?" No one enlightened him but to be in the vicinity of two one ton shells falling with absolute accuracy on a target must have given him a lifetime memory.

The rocket ships had ceased their barrage shortly before the first Landing Craft hit the beaches. They returned to their mother ships ready for the next phase if there was one. The firing from the Naval ships continued as they could put their shells well in front of the advancing army under the direction of the army artillery spotters. There was an occasional air attack alarm as the enemy attempted to penetrate the fighter cover but except for jettisoned bombs we were in no real danger.

In the middle of the afternoon a Motor Gun Boat came almost alongside. Lord Louis Mountbatten was onboard, immaculately dressed in his white uniform as if he was at a garden party. I am afraid after such a considerable time at sea we looked considerably worse for wear. Philip left the bridge and went down to the upper deck where they exchanged pleasantries across the dividing water. I remember thinking that the sartorial splendour of Mountbatten was certainly not reflected in his nephew at the moment. The gold badge on Philip's hat had a distinct green tinge and the gold braid on one of his sleeves was hanging loosely from a few threads. Mountbatten was in charge of the seaborne aspect of the invasion and as usual his knowledge and meticulous planning had paid off handsomely.

Throughout the day the Landing Craft Infantry and The Landing Craft Tanks made a steady and, thankfully, uninterrupted journey to reinforce the spearhead that had worked it's way inwards. The night previous to the landing the sea had been quite turbulent and some doubts were expressed about the capability of the Landing Craft to be able to operate in the then high running sea. Fortunately the wind had dropped just before dawn and the sea had smoothed out considerably. Many of the soldiers had been quite sea sick and that plus the enormous tension of preparing for battle must have placed an almost unbearable strain on every one of them. We need not have worried, they performed magnificently and as each Landing Craft passed us we wished the men God Speed.

Our day was full of activity with the bombardment, the smoke screen and the occasional aircraft warning. The news from our sector was extraordinarily good with reports of a rapid advance towards Etna without the massive opposition that had been expected. As night fell we were ordered round the coast to carry out night patrol outside the port of Syracuse. We were supposed to carry out a cross over patrol with another destroyer so that as he came down one leg of the patrol area we passed him on the other leg. Naturally the night was pitch black, the conditions that had been picked for the invasion. Radio silence was imposed on us so we could not contact him and we never saw him at all until we had a report that he had been sunk in a bombing attack. I was never able to confirm this or even find out the name of the Destroyer. Subsequent events however made this report believable.

We arrived at our patrol position just after ten at night and set a steady course and speed to cover the area. The stars were quite brilliant and on the bridge it seemed we could see for a considerable distance. We had this so-called RDF (subsequently know as Radar) operating. To all intents and purposes it was useless, all it indicated when an aircraft was in the area was just that. Where it was, how high it was and what was it's bearing from the ship remained a complete mystery. Our only means of detection was our ears and with the speed of the aircraft it was impossible to tell with any accuracy at all where the aircraft was in relation to the ship.

The sea was black except where our passing cut a huge wake that glowed with phosphorescence for as far as the eye could see behind us. It was almost midnight when we detected the sound of aircraft coming towards us. It had the sound of a single aircraft and we waited in anticipation for it to pass over. It didn't, suddenly there was the roar of its engine diving followed by the scream of bombs. The bombs made a line of water spouts about two hundred yards down our starboard side and the noise of their explosion was deafening. To all intents and purposes we were a sitting duck of a target. We could not see him but clearly he could see us due to the turbulence of the wake. We waited for his next run but strangely enough his noise receded in the distance.

There was a hurried conference on the bridge and it was decided that the guns would be loaded for barrage firing. The First Lieutenant (Philip) would fire a Very pistol flare in the direction he thought, by listening, the aircraft was approaching. The barrage would be put up in the direction of the flare. Within less than half an hour came the sound of aircraft, whether it was the same aircraft that had landed and reloaded we will never know. The flare went up on our port side and the barrage firing commenced with every short-range weapon as well pouring shot into the direction of the flare. The tracers from the short-range weapons seemed to put up a deadly curtain. It was no use; within seconds we could hear the screaming sound of the bombs dropping and that cringing feeling that made you want to shrink to nothing. The explosions this time were much nearer and the deadly whistle of shrapnel accompanied by the dull thud as some of it found it's mark in the ship's side seemed all around.

Again the aircraft could be heard going away and it was obvious that we were the target for tonight and they would not stop until we had suffered a fatal hit. It was for all the world like being blindfolded and trying to evade an enemy whose only problem was getting his aim right. There was no doubt in anyone's mind that we could dodge for much longer and a direct hit was inevitable. The engineer arrived on the bridge to report that we had suffered minor shrapnel damage above the water line. One of the oil tanks had been slightly holed and we were leaking a small amount of oil as the ship rolled. For a few moments there was no question but to accept the fact that on the next run or the one after that we had little chance of survival. I had been through so much that the feeling of anger and frustration was as great as the fear I and everyone else felt.

It was less than five minutes after the aircraft had departed and, if the previous space in time was approximately the same; we had about twenty minutes to come up with something. We obviously couldn't steam far in that time, not even far enough to make the aircraft think we had moved. The First Lieutenant went into hurried conversation with the Captain and the next thing I knew a wooden raft was being put together on the upper deck. The speed that the men were moving was incredible for within less than five minutes they launched a raft over the side at each end was fastened a smoke float. When it hit the water the smoke floats were activated and billowing clouds of smoke interspersed with small burst of flame gave a convincing imitation of flaming debris in the water.

The Captain ordered full ahead and we steamed away from the raft for a good five minutes and then he ordered the engines stopped. The tell tale wake subsided and we lay there quietly in the soft darkness and cursed the stars, or at least I did. Quite some time went by until we heard the sound of aircraft engines approaching. In the distance we could see the intermittent flames and the masses of smoke from the raft. The next few minutes were the most tension-racked minutes I think I ever went through.

The sound of the aircraft grew louder until I thought it was directly overhead and screwed up my shoulders in anticipation of the scream of bombs. The next thing was the scream of the bombs but at some distance. The ruse had worked and the aircraft was bombing the raft. I suppose he was under the impression that he had hit us in his last attack and was now finishing the job. We lay there quietly waiting for him to leave, which he did, and in view of the solitary attacks so well spaced apart we were convinced he would not return. This proved to be true. It had been marvellously quick thinking, conveyed to a willing team and put into action as if it had been rehearsed. Some times I look back on this particular incident and in view of everything that came after I wonder what would have happened to the Royal House of Windsor if Philip had not thought of this ruse and carried it out so successfully.

The night went by without further incident except that we never met with the destroyer that should have been on the other leg of the patrol. As dawn was breaking we sighted, on the horizon, a group of ships. We immediately trained our guns on these newcomers and, as to our knowledge, no friendly ships could be in the area, the Captain gave the order to challenge them. This procedure consists of transmitting in the direction of the unknown ship or ships a three-letter code by light.

These codes changed daily and one of my jobs was to keep the code of the day and its answer in a readily available position. I made the signal on the ten-inch signal lamp, which, at a million candlepower, could hardly be missed. Once the transmission is made a report is shouted to the Captain who, after an appropriate interval for the receipt of a reply (usually 15 seconds) orders the guns to open fire. The point is that by making the signal you may have told an enemy that you are an enemy and he won't delay in replying to your transmission with gunfire.

The time passed and I had my binoculars glued on the oncoming ships. I reported no reply and the guns opened up. I saw the shells burst almost alongside the oncoming ships and the next salvo would certainly have been direct hits. One of the ships either to dodge the fall of shot or to Zig Zag turned beam on and I screamed cease firing. The Captain ordered the cease-fire and of course asked me what was going on. I explained I had a beam silhouette of the vessel and it was a Landing Craft. Sure enough as we steamed towards them we could see a small group of Landing Craft making for shore and behind them their mother ships who had been beyond our vision over the horizon.

As we closed the Captain asked the lead vessel over the loud hailer if we had caused any casualties and thank heaven the answer was no. He then asked why they had not replied to the challenge and was told they had not been issued with one. It seems that we were not the only one cursed with a Sub Lieut. Smith. In answer to the question "Are we on course," the Captain replied, "Follow the golden trail," we were leaking a small quantity of oil as we moved along and it had spread in our wake leaving a clearly discernible path into the harbour.

CHAPTER TWENTY-THREE

Malta Here We Come - Again!

The engineer together with the shipwright and some of the hands plugged the holes by putting a stage over the side and hammering in plugs. There were not many holes and the job was completed in a very short time. We got underway again and were heading back to join the main body of destroyers. A message was passed to us to join up with several ships that had discharged their precious cargo and escort them to Casablanca. We groaned inwardly as we had already been out of fresh provisions for several days, our water supply was rationed due to the poor distilling capacity and salt water only could be used for washing and bathing. Have you ever tried shaving in seawater? Not pleasant at all!

We passed a destroyer going in to join the flotilla and the Captain drafted a signal for me to send which reported the low state of our ammunition, our fuel oil, our water, the temporary repair that had been carried out and added incidentally the status of our food supply. This was taken by the destroyer and passed by light to the Senior Officer when he joined up with him. The next morning we received a message on the broadcast to leave the convoy and proceed to Malta. With great glee we turned away and headed for Malta where we were ordered in to the destroyer anchorage. Despite the horrible pounding that Malta had taken, from our vantage point the place looked untouched except for the sunken ships that littered the harbour.

There was a tremendous amount of coming and going between the Command centre ashore and the ship. The Captain and First Lieutenant seemed to be making visits on everyone from the C in C downwards. The provisioning lighter came alongside and started to transfer food. From somewhere they had produced rack after rack of fresh bread and nothing in the world at that time could smell any better. The dockyard repair people came out and surveyed the damage and decided the repairs could be made without going into dock. This was a bit of a disappointment as we had hoped to get a few days when we could go ashore. The German intelligence seemed remarkably good as the previous night Lord Haw Haw had announced by name that the Wallace had been sunk. Naturally this message created a great deal of upset back home but fortunately Admiralty immediately denied it over the BBC. There is no question that the Lord Haw Haw broadcasts has some impact at first but by this time people in Britain knew that most of his broadcasts were lies and half truths.

We did get ashore in Malta in the next four days. The Maltese are wonderful people whose courage and fortitude had been demonstrated many time throughout the ages against foreign invaders. They are a happy band of people under normal circumstances and this is one of the few places where they recognise and appreciate the fact that in peace and in war, the navy was their greatest financial support. I had been to Malta many times and I fully expected the bombing and the hardships would have wreaked an awful toll on the island and the people. I was astounded to find how quickly everything had returned to normal despite the damage. I went to Valletta to that area known as "The Gut" fully expecting a street of ruins. Instead there they were, pretty girls standing in the doorways of café's, bars and small cabaret's with their familiar cry of "Here sailor, this is the place," and "Inside Jack and meet the girls."

The shortage of food on the island had been horrific and caused tremendous suffering. Once the gauntlet had been run and the deadlock broken tons of food and supplies were poured into the island and already some of the small restaurants were back in business with, of course, a limited menu. My friends and I went into one and sat with a cold beer. The waiter asked if we would like a steak. We were really amazed but we said yes and shortly four huge steaks still sizzling were set in front of us. We set to with a will, as fresh meat to us was something we dreamed about. When we pushed our plates away, totally satisfied the Coxswain said, "That was the best piece of horse meat I have ever eaten." He was right as the waiter told us, large shipments of horsemeat had been among the first of the supplies to arrive. I often wonder if I had known would I have eaten it. I think the answer is yes I would. I have never (knowingly) eaten horsemeat again.

Back onboard the mail had arrived. Many letters were missing in the series we had established but nevertheless it was a delight to know what was happening and how everyone was keeping. It was quite incredible how much, without mentioning the war, we had in common to talk about. Censorship made war talk impossible but frankly we did not miss it as we were full of plans for the future. The ship was ready within four days and fully provisioned together with ammunition, oil and fresh water we sailed for home. The journey back went without incident but of course we were constantly on the alert. We called into Gibraltar and we managed to spend a few pleasant hours ashore indulging in our favourite occupation, eating and drinking.

The trip across the Bay of Biscay was unusually calm and a few days later we saw the familiar sights and headed for the Firth of Forth like a homing pigeon. We arrived alongside, there was no guard and band, no trumpets, no welcoming bunch of shore bound Admirals, no visitors. Only a lonely dockyard hand that caught our heaving line and pulled our cable ashore secured it and ran aft to do the same there. I suppose I was expecting too much but somehow I had in my mind that somewhere someone in authority would recognise "The warrior from the war returning" as the book says, and at least have a couple of welcoming people on the Jetty.

It was truly an anti climax and I know that everyone on the ship felt let down. After we had secured the order was given to stop main engines, die down in boilers not required and the pipe meaning stand down echoed around the ship. For the first time in weeks the ship was still, no vibration, no side to side and up and down roll and lift. We sat alongside each other at the mess table and realised that we could not all sit at once, it was too crowded. It was the first time in months that at least a third of the mess was not away on duty or on watch.

No one suggested it to my knowledge but there appeared on the table a selection of glasses and a full bottle of "Pussers" rum. The Coxswain poured a good tot for each of us and when he had finished we picked up the glasses, looked at one another, clinked glasses and without a word being spoken we downed the rum. I will never forget that moment, nothing needs to be said, no words could do our feelings justice, and we were in magnificent company.

CHAPTER TWENTY-FOUR

Worn Out

It was the end of August 1943 when we again picked up the routine we had left to take part in greater endeavours. I have to admit that invasion and all; it had not only been a welcome change of routine but in fact, far less nerve wracking. Except for the incident with the bomber off Sicily, we had encountered in the whole trip and invasion less action than we normally encountered on a single convoy down the East coast.

We, naturally, were somewhat reluctant to pick up the gauntlet again but there was no alternative offered. As usual we picked the convoy up at Methil and were somewhat amused and not a little flattered to receive welcome back messages, not only from the convoy Commodore, but also from some of the ships that were our regulars. We learned later that some of the regulars were convinced that they were better off in a convoy of which we were escort than any other. Sailor's superstition again I expect but nevertheless it made us feel good.

Although we encountered the usual bombing runs etc., it seemed to us that the heart had gone out of the opposition. They did not seem to press home their attacks with the remembered vigour and certainly the machine gun strafing did not occur. The fact that we had first class fighter cover we could call on and receive an immediate response may, to some extent, explain their attitude. We however convinced ourselves that the armed forces of Germany could already see the writing on the wall. In the next three months we lost ships to E Boat attacks and to mines but bombing casualties were few and far between.

We started spending more and more time tied up to the jetty in Rosyth. Breakdowns of equipment were more frequent, boilers were not responding to the regular cleaning and more and more repairs to keep us fit for sea had to be carried out. I took advantage of my knowledge of what was happening and going to happen and brought my wife to Rosyth whenever we were going to spend four or more days alongside. We booked into a small hotel in Dunfermline, a small town not too far from Rosyth. She came onboard several times during these visits and met the men I had lived with in such close quarters all these years. The Coxswain made a great fuss of her and they became great friends. When she came onboard for dinner it was made into quite an event and we all had some great evenings and as she was invariably the only woman, she loved the attention. The Coxswain's hobby was making leather goods and he made her a leather handbag that was a work of art. She treasured it for many years.

We were invited down to the Wardroom where she met all the officers including Philip and she was quite a hit with them. On a couple of occasions when we were leaving the ship to go back to the hotel by taxi, Philip asked if he could join us on his way to the railway station. The two of them would enter into an animated conversation about something and his attention and courtesy made her feel really good.

It became obvious that, to maintain any kind of fighting efficiency, the ship needed a major refit. She was literally worn out, gun barrels needed replacing, leaks around the portholes constantly flooding the messdeck, generators breaking down, these and many other things made it obvious that we were coming to the end of our journey together. It was decided in December to pay her off and put her in refit. I found out later that the refit took a full eight months to complete.

It was a bleak day in January 1944 when the ship's company was fallen in for the last time. There were the usual speeches from attending senior officers full of fulsome praise for our courage and endurance. They fell on deaf ears; we had no illusions left. They had no concept of how we felt on this occasion. They did not realise, or they seemed not to realise, the enormity of what was happening. Standing around me were men with whom I must now part company. Men who had become so close that they formed the only world I had known for over three years. Men who had gone through hell so many times and now had to listen to platitudes about comrades in arms and loyalty and bravery from people who did not know the meaning of the words. We were impatient to get it over with and the shuffling of feet, coughing and restlessness conveyed this attitude in unmistakable terms resulting in a cutting short of this ceremony.

I gave the Coxswain a hand in preparing the travel documents for the ship's company. They were being well spread out to their home ports, Devonport, Chatham, Portsmouth and other establishments for the specialists. In this way I saw and spoke to every member of the ship's company individually when they lined up to get their papers. It was a typical male concealment of any feelings of sentiment. A few gruff words, a shake of the hand and a rapid turn away. Wiggy came along with his cohorts and we went through the same routine with one minor, but to me, major difference. As he turned away he said, "Slongers your alright, I'm alright." We both roared with laughter to the total mystification of everyone around us.

I went directly on leave for ten days, incredible as it may seem this was the longest leave I had since the war started. To say I enjoyed it would be the understatement of my life. My orders were to report to the Signal School in Devonport on completion.

CHAPTER TWENTY-FIVE

Back to School

I arrived back at the Signal School which was a Holiday Camp taken over for the duration of the war. I went through the usual entry routine and was allocated one of the Chalet's that had been used to house two holidaymakers. I was its only occupant and to me it seemed palatial. It was heated by a pot-bellied wood stove and there was a supply of wood stacked outside the door.

The Chief and Petty Officers mess was a large Nissen Hut that, once inside, had every possible amenity. Snooker tables, Dartboards, a long bar and a small kitchen where the food that came from the central galley was served. I knew several of the people already there and I looked forward to a period of rest and relaxation. Some of us spent my first evening over a drink exchanging our different stories of how we had occupied our time since the beginning of the war. Everything that day seemed normal to me and I left them to turn in around ten that night.

That night the nightmares started. I woke up to find myself frantically scrabbling to get my clothes on in a desperate fit of fear. It took me a while to come round and realise where I was. I was bathed in a cold sweat and shaking as if I would never stop. I turned back in and lay there shivering until, with almost a physical effort, I forced myself to stop shivering. I finally went off to sleep. I did not mention it to anyone the next day as I regarded it as a passing dream.

The day passed with all the normal routine and that night I turned in having dismissed the previous night's incident as an aberration. That night when a nightmare came I did not wake up until it had run itself through like a horror movie. I was lying on the deck of the bridge looking up into the sun. I could see aircraft moving slowly across the sky blacking out the sun. I could hear the scream of bombs falling and then I saw two bombs dropping vertically side-by-side coming straight down on me. I rolled over on my face and felt myself almost burrowing into the deck then I awoke and I was on my face in the bed frantically scrabbling at the mattress. Again I was soaked with perspiration and my heartbeat was so fast it seemed to be jumping out of my chest. It took ages before I could sleep.

In the days that followed I had no real duty to perform, as I was supernumerary as they called it. In other words I was there waiting a further draft to some other ship or depot. The nightmares continued, the most recurring dream was the falling bombs. I started to walk around until I was exhausted at night, sometimes not turning in until two and three in the morning but it did not help. After two weeks of sleeping very little and not eating properly I realised I had to do something. I went to the sick bay and had an interview with the Doctor.

He turned out to be a very pleasant young man who had recently completed all the necessary things to become a fully-fledged G.P. He had joined the navy and been given the rank of Lieutenant automatically. I found out he had never even seen a destroyer never mind served in one. In fact he had not done one day onboard any ship. This rather stultified our conversation as I, without thinking, used naval expressions in describing things. While he was a willing listener he simply could not, even in his wildest imagination, come to grips with the facts of war at sea.

He suggested that I needed rest away from the naval environment and said he could authorise seven days leave. With weekends this would be ten days and I jumped at the suggestion. Within hours I had my travel documents and ration cards and was on my way to the rail station. The days of telephones in every house had not yet come and on all previous occasions a telegram would get home before me. My arrival therefor was a complete, and for both of us, a wonderful surprise.

We stayed up late talking about everything as usual. My wife was concerned when I told her the story but we both felt that this break would be all I needed. That night I really scared her. She woke me up as I was desperately trying to open a door that wasn't there. I did not remember the dream that had caused it but again I was soaked in sweat with an extremely rapid heartbeat. This continued on during my leave. I would sleep during the day sitting in an armchair, anything to avoid the nightmares.

I reported back and went straight to see the Doctor. I told him what had happened and what was still happening. He decided to send me immediately over to the naval hospital in Plymouth. They laid on transport and I arrived in mid afternoon with instructions to see a certain specialist. This Doctor held the rank of Commander and had obviously seen sea time during the war. He talked to me for over an hour constantly asking questions and writing down the replies. He then arranged for me to stay in the hospital overnight and made an appointment for me at nine in the morning.

I had an early supper and turned in. I was in a ward with four beds all of them occupied. A Nurse came in and gave me a couple of pills she said were a sedative the Doctor had ordered. The next thing I was aware of was being heavily shaken and told to wake up. There was a nurse and the duty doctor at my bedside. According to them I had woken up the ward by shouting but they could not make out what I was saying. I did not remember any dream but I was bathed in sweat and shivering. They moved me to a single room for the rest of the night.

The interview the next day was the Commander and two civilian doctors. It lasted until lunch time and it seemed as if they had asked every question possible. I must say they were extremely thorough and arranged for a further interview at three the same afternoon. When the time arrived it seemed the whole tenor of the interview had changed. Their questions were asked in a much gentler manner and there was no feeling of aggression or scepticism. In fact, the only word I can use was respectful; they were more respectful.

Towards the end of the session the Commander asked if I had kept in touch with any of my former shipmates. I said I had written and as we had not been apart for long and the mail would have to be forwarded to them from their home address I had not received any replies. He then told me he had not only been in touch with my last Captain but also the one before. They were both serving in shore jobs and he had spoken to them on the telephone. He said that both of them had asked if I needed anything and that they would like him to keep them informed. I felt really good about this piece of news.

This little medical committee decided I needed at least a month away from everything and to this end I was sent to a convalescent hospital away in the country. It turned out to be one of the stately homes of England made available by a Lord Cholmondely (pronounced Chumleigh). It was magnificent with rolling parkland and woodland, a stream running through and far away from any traffic. The staff was the epitome of kindness and every consideration was given to making us comfortable. The main rooms were large and airy and the bedrooms were luxurious although, of course, I had to share with three others.

The change was so complete I was sure the peaceful surroundings would make a tremendous difference to my state of mind, at least, on that first day looking at everything I convinced myself it would. It did not happen and that night I woke the other three in the room by shouting and bouncing about in my bed. The night duty nurse came in and woke me up and I awoke to a room fully lit with all the other occupants sitting up looking at me. I felt awful and, although I don't know why, I felt ashamed of myself and wondered how I could go on like this. The next day I told the doctor who interviewed me about this feeling and he became almost angry. "Never" he said, and he repeated it several times, "Never let that feeling even cross your mind, it is destructive and totally unjustified". I thought to myself that it was easy enough for him to say but he hadn't looked in the faces of people who had been wakened during the night by someone having nightmares.

During the day I wandered aimlessly through the beautiful grounds. I did not want to talk to anyone; in fact I did not want to see anyone. All I could think of was the fact that my performance would be the subject of discussion and curiosity. I should have known better as every patient in the place had a problem of his own and was not really interested in discussing mine. However, I suppose most people in my position would be cursed with an over active imagination.

After lunch an orderly came for me and told me I had an appointment now and would I go with him to the office. When I entered, sitting at the desk was one of the civilian doctors whom I had seen at the original medical committee. He stood up and shook hands. He asked me to sit on the opposite side of the desk. He explained that he was on the permanent staff of this place and only went to the hospital for, as he put it, "Screening purposes". He must have been twice my age, hair turning slightly grey and thinning on top, a rumpled jacket that looked like Harris Tweed that had seen better days, slightly portly with a ruddy face and a very pleasant smile.

"Now" he said, "I am going to call you Harry and you are going to call me Ben, is that all right?" I said it was, and then he explained what the routine was going to be. As he talked I saw him glance at my hands that were resting on the table. He pointed to them and asked how long had that been going on. "That" was the fact that where my hands rested there was a pool of perspiration on the desk. I told him it had started just a few weeks ago and it made me too embarrassed to shake hands, as they were always cold and wet. He told me not to worry about it, as it would soon be cleared up. I hoped he was right.

He arranged that we would meet either in the garden or the conservatory depending on the weather at 2 O'clock every day. During the rest of the time he prescribed different activities such as walking, cycling, swimming and quiet times for reading. The nights had not improved but under his orders I had been given a small room with myself as the only occupant.

Our first meeting was so casual it was like two friends out for a companionable walk. I am sure he talked as much as I did but as the days went by I realised that he was delving deeply into my last few years, particularly the time I had spent in the Wallace. He was a stickler for dates and on many occasions I could only give him an approximate time when certain things happened. He seemed extraordinarily interested in the times people had joined and left the ship. He was fascinated and laughed with me over Wiggy and his adventures. He made me repeat stories that I had told him only a few days before and had me enlarge on them and fill in the natural gaps that you skip over when telling a story.

Some times I expressed my reluctance to elaborate on some incidents. "How did you feel," he would say "when you had to go through water in which survivors were swimming and leave them behind?" He asked, "if I resented the decision to do this or any other such incident." I had to answer him that quite honestly I didn't. I knew it was necessary. I had told him about the invasion of Sicily and he asked why I had such a feeling of horror when the rocket ships fired into the enemy. I couldn't explain that except to say that it seemed, at the moment, so one sided.

These conversations went on every day, sometimes lasting only an hour, sometimes the whole afternoon. He made no changes in my routine; he made no suggestions about anything I should be doing differently. Meanwhile the nightmares recurred but I was beginning to cope with them better by realising in the first moment of conscious thought, that it was a dream. Two weeks had passed and I really was beginning to wonder where all this was leading, I certainly wasn't improving much.

Then, one day, he asked me how I felt about my problem. I tried to explain to him that I felt terribly self-conscious about it; I told him I did not want to use the word, ashamed, but that is how I felt sometimes. We were walking through the park at the time and he gestured for us to sit on a park bench. "Well" he said, "do you realise that you were the only person in that ship who spent three whole years exposed on that bridge while at sea? I have checked all the dates and, including the Captains, the next longest was a year and a half." I had to admit that it had never crossed my mind as the transitions from one person to another was a gradual process one at a time with intervals between.

Strangely enough I seemed to find some peace of mind in that fact. It, for some reason, took away some of the feeling of guilt that had been bothering me. The next day I asked him if he, in his research, had found any other member of the ship's company hospitalised. He said he could not discuss that with me. That night the nightmare changed to something less terrifying although still very disturbing. I was in a ship lying alongside a jetty in some port. I had gone ashore on my own and was walking through the streets of this strange port as darkness fell. I decided to retrace my steps to the ship. I suddenly realised I did not know where I was and what was worse I could not remember the name of my ship or where she was berthed. I did not know enough to be able to ask an intelligent question of passers by. The feeling of panic rose as I realised I was completely lost. At this point I awoke, sweating as usual but not crying out this time.

I told him about the dream the next day and he seemed pleased with the change but did not or could not explain why, I was in my third week and was getting very anxious about the future. My wife's letters came regularly and I replied telling her I was having a decent rest and relaxation. Neither of us mentioned the dreams. It must have been a worrying time for her.

The "Lost Dream" as I came to refer to it, recurred but the other dreams seem to have receded. It was three days before another "Bomb Dream" occurred and I was devastated as I thought they had gone. When I told him about this recurrence he almost smiled. "Well Harry", he said, "I think we have a handle on the problem." He explained that for the last week a strict policy of silence had been enforced around my room after I had gone to sleep. The very first night of this complete undisturbed silence my dream had changed. Three days later, or should I say nights, while he was observing me sleeping he had the nurse rattle some trays together. Within seconds I was wide-awake shaking, trembling and sweating.

His theory, and it proved to be right, was that my violent reaction to an unfamiliar noise was calling my mind to "Action Stations". My nightmare apparently only lasted a few seconds but long enough to plunge me back into a situation that had made a horrible impact on my mind. His prescription was easy and it worked beyond my wildest hope.

Before turning in I had to drink a glass of warm milk. A small light had to be left on enough to show me when I awoke, the surroundings I was in. A radio tuned very low to create a background noise that some how assured my mind that I was in safe surroundings.

It did not of course work immediately although the bomb dream did not come back. After a few days the "Lost Dream" failed to appear and the next two weeks were spent in these idyllic surroundings and able to thoroughly enjoy them. Ben tried to explain the problem but he did admit that he had gone through trial and error and as he put it "Sheer guesswork" to find the cause. He believed that I had become so accustomed to my environment onboard that anything out of, what was to me ordinary, rang alarm bells.

Ringing the alarm bells was, to me, exposure to something that was life threatening against which I had to react. He had tested my reaction time to conventional things, such as how fast I pushed a button when a certain coloured light went on and other physical tests. He told me that I reacted in less than half the time the average person would take. In other words, when I was awake or sleeping I was on edge.

Today I find it almost impossible to describe the feeling of relief when the cause and then the cure were discovered. During the dark days I had been wondering what the future held. What was I going to do to support a family, how could they cope with me and these frightening (for them) episodes? This had led to bouts of depression that Ben assured me would not recur, and he was right. To this day, however, the routine of the milk and when possible the music has become a standard routine although since leaving there I have never had a recurrence in these many years.

One thing that had been bothering me I had to clear up to my own satisfaction. While I accepted Ben's explanation about the long and continuous exposure being the cause of my problem, was I the only one. The letters we wrote to each other had started to arrive on a regular basis. In them were of course details of the life my friends were living. I did not want, or even dare, to ask direct questions that would have satisfied my curiosity. I had to read between the lines and sure enough three or four had either been in hospital or under a Doctors care. When sympathised with accompanied by jokes about whose stairs they had fallen down none of them discussed the cause of their hospitalisation or the need for the Doctor's care.

As far as the officers were concerned it was relatively easy to find out what appointments they had when leaving the ship. I found a strange hiatus between appointments with unexplainable gaps. Some of them had been shore bound for over 8 months with no actual appointment recorded against them. This research left me satisfied that, even if I was barking up the wrong tree, there was ample evidence to convince me that I was not unique in this breakdown.

I said goodbye to Ben, he had done so much for me and I was grateful beyond mere words. He waved away my thanks and told me that even without his help the problem would have gone away, he merely put it in perspective, which brought it to a solution a little earlier than it would have taken. I never heard from him or saw him again although I did write but received no reply. I assumed he had moved on to other more pressing problems and in any case could not occupy his time in writing to ex patients which, if my experience was any measure, there would be quite a few.

CHAPTER TWENTY-SIX

Just Desserts

I returned to the Depot with written instructions to be sent on three weeks leave. I checked in with the Chief at the regulating office and he greeted me warmly. We sat around for a while talking and he allocated me the same Chalet as before. He asked me to go into the inner office out of earshot of the wren typist and the messenger. He closed the door and told me the reason for his not wanting to be heard. "The last time you were here," he said, "The X.O. (executive officer) was on leave." He then went on to warn me about this officer.

He told me that this officer had retired early in the year when war broke out. He had been called back in and, in fact, had taken this depot over from the Holiday camp owners and turned it into what it was today; a transient depot for people like myself, a holding depot for new entries until they could be accommodated in the main depots and a demobilisation facility for those being discharged from the service.

I found this interesting but not unusual until he started on about the character of the man. He flatly stated he was a sadistic bully who terrorised the new recruits, and the wrens. He treated the Chief and Petty Officers with absolute contempt except for a couple of sycophants. He asked me if I knew "Burglar Johnson." I told him I had met him once but I was fully aware of the reason they called him "burglar". The explanation was, that this Chief Petty Officer had retired under a cloud two years before the war. He had gone into business with a civilian partner and literally robbed him into bankruptcy by selling inventory without recording it and pocketing the money. He was prosecuted and sent to jail. However, the sentence had been such that he did not lose his pension and was called up with the rest of the eligible pensioners when war was declared. According to the Chief, this was the X.O.'s right hand man.

I knew that wherever this man went he left a train of unproveable offences behind. Everything from motor bikes to raincoats vanished, everybody knew the culprit but proving it was something else. He had been sent from depot to depot finishing up here where it appeared as if he had fallen in with a kindred spirit. I listened to his story and sympathised. It was Thursday and I was going on leave on Monday and frankly, I simply could not be bothered getting into someone else's problems. Little did I realise that in that short time I would have problems of my own.

The normal routine when joining a ship or establishment is to join the requestmen and defaulters at the routine time in the morning. Normally you would be first in line, introduced to the X.O. who had your documents in front of him. He could then put a face to the documents and welcome you onboard. On Friday morning I appeared in the drill shed where about a dozen or so requestment and defaulters were lined up waiting their turn. I took the head of the queue and waited for my name to be called. The X.O. appeared closely followed by "Burglar" Johnson and two others.

The regulating chief stood at the lectern awaiting his arrival. My first glimpse of the man was all I needed to place him in his category. He was a big sloppy individual with a bloated pink face and the fair eyelashes and blue eyes that were almost pig like. His jowls shook as he spoke and his fingers looked like sausages as he waved his hand and pointed to emphasise some point. Shades of Ganges, I thought, he had all the signs.

There was a little discussion when he arrived and I was surprised to hear the name of a Petty Officer called who had joined the depot the same day as myself. Under normal circumstances I should have gone ahead of him. He stepped smartly up to the lectern and saluted, this was totally ignored. The X.O. then launched into an incredible diatribe about discipline, how he ran a tight ship and the way the Chiefs and Petty Officers let him down. Although he was addressing the Petty Officer I noticed he constantly glanced at me to make sure I was getting the message. He finished by warning the Petty Officer that if he stepped out of line he would be back at sea within twenty four hours.

My name was called and I stepped up and saluted and was totally ignored. He was reading the top letter on my file. "Another dodger, eh?" he said. I couldn't believe my ears and opened my mouth to speak. "Keep silent when I am speaking," he practically spat at me. "I will make sure you don't get on this so called sick leave," he said. "I'll have you at sea where dodgers like you belong." I was speechless and furious while the requestmen and defaulters listened with great interest. I saw the Chief shaking his head trying to tell me not to say anything to make matters worse. "Burglar Johnson" had a smirk on his face while the others looked everywhere except at me. He then went into a similar diatribe about keeping a tight ship etc., etc.

When he had finished he indicated this by a dismissal wave of his hand. I saluted, turned away and walked out of the drill shed. I honestly could have killed him. The youngsters listening had no knowledge of me or my background so must assume the worst. The Chief's were for some reason totally intimidated by this man and would not correct the impression. I went to the regulating office and waited for the Chief to arrive. I occupied my time by filling out the formal request to see the Captain to state a complaint.

The Chief arrived and immediately apologised for the treatment I had received. "He is like that with every new Chief that arrives," he said. "He makes their lives so miserable that they request a draft anywhere and he sees they get it," I said, "Well here's a request that won't please him at all." The Chief took it, read it and his face turned white, "Please" he said, "don't do this." I asked him why not and it was obvious that he too was terrified of the man.

He left the office and went over to the X.O.'s office. A few minutes later he returned with the request torn up in small pieces. I sat down and wrote another one and gave it to him when he handed me the torn pieces. I told him to take it back and tell the X.O. that if he tore up this one I would deliver another one personally to the Captain. Poor Chief, he looked so terribly upset but he had no recourse but to go. The office was next door and I heard the roar of anger as the Chief delivered the message.

When he returned I asked him for the list of people who had been at the table including the Chiefs. I also told him to notify everyone on the list to be outside the Captain's office on Monday morning ready to be called as witnesses. I thought he was going to have a heart attack at this news. He left me and went straight to the X.O's cabin. It was some time later when he returned and he told me that the X.O. had spoken hastily and through the Chief, he apologised. I told him that I would not accept an apology unless given in front of all who had heard the insult. He again made the trip but when he came back he told me the X.O. would make sure my complaint would not get me anywhere.

Over the weekend I pondered on this strange situation and was completely puzzled. Why was everyone so terrified of this man. How could a known criminal be treated as a trusted ally. I wondered about the Captain, according to the Chief he had only been there a month and only appeared at Sunday Divisions (this is a parade where all the ship's company are mustered on the parade ground). I didn't even know the Captain's name and the Chief hadn't enlightened me. Under normal circumstances making a complaint directed at an officer was a very serious business and the complainant had better be absolutely sure of his grounds. It is inevitable that the officers close ranks against anyone from the lower deck. I knew this but my state of mind at this time was such that I simply could not care what happened. I had endured enough and did not intend to take anymore.

Monday morning came and at breakfast in the mess there was a general air of doom and gloom. The Chief spoke to me but no one else. He told me that all the people that were present at the incident had been told to appear. I was dressed in my best uniform with gold badges etc., etc. As far as I was concerned, when this fiasco was over I was going on leave. As I left the mess he walked a little way with me. "I want to warn you" he said, "that all the people who will be there have been visited by "Burglar Johnson" over the week end." I had not expected that but to me it was a real plus.

There were enough of them to elicit the fact that they had been threatened from at least one or two of them. I made my way over to stand outside the Chalet that the Captain used as an office. There was a wide-open window above my head and I could hear the voices inside quite clearly. The other people I had insisted on being present were there in a queue except, of course, the sycophants.

The X.O. with his retinue arrived but they stayed outside while he went in to brief the Captain. I could hear every word and if it hadn't been serious it would have been laughable. I was mutinous, I despised authority, I encouraged disobedience among the ratings, I was dodging going to sea and because he had caught me I had put in this frivolous complaint. He advised the Captain to summarily dismiss the complaint and see me as a defaulter for disobedience of orders.

The Captain wanted to know how long this activity of mine had been going on. The X.O. blustered and tried to avoid the question. His blustering was interrupted by the Captain. "According to his documents he did not join this depot until three days ago, he must have been very busy to accumulate all your charges." The X.O. then said, "I know him by his reputation, Chief Johnson thoroughly briefed me so I immediately let him know I was aware of his dodging."

The Captain told the Chief who had been there throughout this diatribe, to bring me in. I heard my name called and entered the office, stood to attention and saluted. I could hardly believe my eyes. Sitting behind the desk having risen to the full rank of Captain was a Captain I had served with at the beginning of the war; he was a Lieutenant Commander then. "I thought I recognised the name," he said with a smile. " I read your service documents last night, you have certainly been busy since we last met." The X.O. stood there with his mouth practically hanging open.

He started to speak but the Captain angrily waved him to silence. "Now," he said, "What is this all about?" I described in detail the diatribes and the incident at the table, the tearing up of requests, (I produced the torn up pieces) and how the list of witnesses had been threatened by Chief Johnson. I inadvertently referred to him as "Burglar Johnson" which elicited an enquiry from the Captain about the origin of the nickname. I was delighted to oblige, to the attempted furious interruptions of the X.O. The Captain advised the X.O. that if he did not wish to be present he had his permission to leave.

The Captain asked me what steps had to be taken to satisfy my justifiable complaint. I told him I was due to go on leave that day and was anxious to get this whole thing over with. I explained about all the people who were present at the incident were outside if I needed witnesses. The Captain shook his head to indicate this was not required. I then said if I received an apology from the X.O. in front of all the people who had been at the table I would consider the incident closed. The X.O. shook his head until his jowls literally trembled; he went red in the face. "My authority on this base will be totally undermined," he protested, "I admit I spoke hastily and I am prepared to apologise privately." The Captain raised his eyebrows in enquiry and I shook my head, "That's not good enough sir," I said, "The people out there will never believe any different unless they hear the apology." "Then I have no recourse but to pass this on to the Admiral for his decision," the Captain said.

The X.O.'s face went from red to white, I have never seen such a change in my life. He stuttered and stammered but finally he pulled himself together and said in a shaking voice "We don't want to bother the Admiral with this. I will apologise as he," here he glared at me, "Wishes." The Chief mustered everyone at the door below the three entrance steps including the sycophants. The Captain said, "The Chief has requested that you hear this." The X.O. stepped forward but before he could speak I recalled to them the words used by the X.O. and how they constituted a terrible insult for which the X.O. would now apologise.

I pointed out it was not a mistake or a case of mistaken identity. This took the wind out of his sails as I had left him with no excuse. He said that he sincerely apologised and would make sure such an incident would not occur again. He then turned to me and held out his hand, which I ignored and walked back into the office. The Captain told me to stay and had the office cleared. We talked about old ships and incidents; he was fascinated by the tales of the East Coast convoys. He then asked what did I think of the depot he had just taken over. I told him how puzzled I was at the fear the X.O. had instilled into everyone particularly the Chiefs. I couldn't understand how "Burglar Johnson" could be in such a position of trust that he practically ran the place. I had only been there three days yet it was obvious something was radically wrong.

I left his office and went immediately to the regulating office to collect my travel warrants and ration cards. The Chief had them all ready and with a beaming countenance he wished me well in my travels and shook my hand as if he wanted to keep it. After that it was all down hill. The transport, the train home and three weeks glorious leave.

There was of course a sequel to all this but I only heard of it second hand many months later. It appears that the X.O. had bought a farm to retire to when the war ended. It needed a great deal of renovation to be habitable. Naval stores with it's stocks of wood, paint and every conceivable item was the ideal place to draw on for materials. The fact that it was illegal didn't phase "Burglar Johnson" one bit and the X.O. was delighted to find such a cheap and unrationed source as "Burglar Johnson" for all his needs.

The supply of rationed meat under the counter to a couple of local butcher shops was uncovered, meat taken from the rations of the men in the Depot. Again "Burglar Johnson" was the instigator although he tried to push it on to the civilian caterer. I felt the worst offence however were the payoffs arranged between the Chief running the drafting office and those in the depot. They paid him a monthly fee to make sure their draft cards for service at sea were never brought forward. I now understood why transients like myself were quickly ousted from the depot under any excuse.

Apparently there was no public scandal. Not even a courts martial. The people involved were either prematurely retired or dispersed around the fleet, several finishing in distant places. This may not seem right but it is understandable. The Captain of the depot would have been held responsible and the people in charge of the drafting office would have been dragged in. Burglar Johnson and his coterie escaped the severe punishment they deserved as the careers of many totally innocent people could have been ruined. It would have been different if they had even the slightest inkling of what was happening but "Burglar Johnson" did not get his nickname for nothing.

CHAPTER TWENTY-SEVEN

Back to School

Leave passes too quickly and it seemed no time at all before I was back in the depot waiting whatever the fates decreed. It was only two days and I was on my way to Northern Ireland to look after communications at a naval air station. The Normandy invasion was taking place and I could envision, all too clearly, the terrible battle conditions that would be prevailing. I felt very peculiar about what was going on; detached, I think, would be the best description. I was surrounded by people who, due to their role in the scheme of things, spoke a different war language than mine. Theirs encompassed war at a distance no less hazardous, no less vital but nevertheless much less of a hands on affair.

I had settled in to what, to me, was a humdrum existence. Except for the occasional emergency landing at the air base and the constant communication with the American Flying Fortress aircraft, who, incidentally signalled their intention to land on our runway and had to be dissuaded most firmly. The runway was hardly more than the length of an aircraft carrier's deck and any aircraft of that size would certainly end up in the mountain at the end of the runway. They gave us some anxious moments.

I received the news that my brother had been killed in France after successfully landing and getting inland with his regiment. I hit an all time low with this news. My Father had been killed in the First World War and, as it turned out, very near where my brother died. The impact on me was bad but I knew my mother would be torn apart. He left a wife and a small son and try as I might I find it is impossible to look upon the German people, who, let's face it, were totally responsible for this war, with any kind of tolerance.

After a few months I was drafted to a division of the Western Approaches Command in Milford Haven. I was now back in the atmosphere with which I was so familiar. Convoys were still running, U Boats were still fighting but losing the battle and the messages that passed through my hands told of the beginning of the end.

The war in Europe ended followed by the war in the Pacific. I was sent back to depot and simply did not know what to expect. Demobilisation of the men and women called up for the hostilities was in full swing. Everywhere ships were being paid off and the Naval

Barracks were overflowing with people to an extent it was almost unbelievable. I only spent a few days and was sent for to be briefed on another draft.

This time I was being sent out to the Far East with tasks to perform in the Naval Shore stations that had been reactivated when taken back from the Japanese. I was informed that my absence would only be for one year, therefore, under the regulations, I could not bring my wife to whichever base I finally settled in. Naturally the idea of another years absence hit us both hard. My wife believed at the time, and she turned out to be totally correct, that once I was out there they would find excuses to keep me on the job longer than the promised year.

I thought I was in luck when I received orders to join a passenger Liner that was taking replacements out to the same area. The day before I was due to leave the orders were changed and I had to join the Aircraft Carrier Formidable, which was being used as a passenger ferry. The hanger had been divided into temporary sections with bunks and was undoubtedly the most uncomfortable design that some moron could come up with. The reason for my transfer was that three officers were taking passage, one commander and two lieut commanders. They were relieving the commanding officers of destroyers based on Hong Kong. My job was to give them daily instructions in the Conduct of the Fleet; the manual that contains all the rules for manoeuvring and screening ships.

They were nice people but I was astonished at their total lack of experience in this vital subject and their poor knowledge of destroyer life in general. I had no way of finding out their background or past experience but I was of the opinion that they were either products of the big ships or had been shore bound in operation rooms. Two months after they left I had a visit from a Lieutenant who was the communication officer of the flotilla. He told me that the Senior Officer of the flotilla, who was the Commander I had instructed, wanted to know if I was interested in going to the Flotilla leader as his Chief Yeoman. I was flattered but declined as I, at that time, was hoping to go home in a few months. As events transpired I should have taken up the offer.

I was called on to do a multitude of tasks in different countries eventually finishing up in Hong Kong. I had to start a communication school from scratch and it was a tremendously difficult and demanding task. Every time I requested to be sent home as my year had expired there was excuse after excuse. It was two and a half years before I saw my family again, two and a half lost years with my daughters and my wife. I never forgave the people responsible for that.

The fact that I carried on and then transferred to the Canadian Navy, finishing my 35-year career as a Lieutenant Commander was due to two factors. The first was that I was totally a sailor; I had no experience with civilian life and what I had seen of it I did not like. The second was that while I was a master of my trade, it was a trade that in those days would never have helped me make a living in civilian life. In the years that followed and remembering this lesson I broadened my horizons so that when I eventually did leave I could earn an excellent living.

Harry Hargreaves

Harry Hargreaves joined the Royal Navy at the age of 15 in 1933. He trained to become a Signal boy. His first posting was to the destroyer H.M.S. Barham. He served with the Royal Navy on a variety of destroyers and saw the introduction of new technologies such as ASDIC and Radar. In 1948 he left the Royal Navy and joined the Canadian Royal Navy; emigrating to Canada with his wife and four daughters. In total Harry has 35 years service with the Navy and retired with the rank of Lieutenant Commander.

Today he lives in Ontario with his beagle, Tabatha. Requests from friends and family to tell the stories of his years in the Navy, inspired him to write these, his memoirs; "Musings of a Matelot", covering the years 1933 through 1945.